THE COLOSSAL KIDS' JOKE BOOK

Published by Arcturus Publishing Limited
26/27 Bickels Yard, 151–153 Bermondsey Street, London SE1 3HA

for Bookmart Limited
Registered Number 2372865
Trading as Bookmart Limited
Desford Road
Enderby
Leicester
LE19 4AD

This edition published 2003

Printed and bound in India

In Canada published for
Indigo Books
468 King St W,
Suite 500,
Toronto,
Ontario M5V 1L8

ISBN 1-84193-174-8

THE COLOSSAL KIDS' JOKE BOOK

PETER COUPE

CONTENTS

CROSSES

What do you get if you cross a
jogger with an apple pie?

Puff Pastry!

What do you get if you cross a sheep and a space ship ?

Apollo neck woolly jumpers !

What do you get if you cross a pig
with a naked person ?

Streaky bacon !

What do you get if you cross a box of
matches and a giant ?

The big match !

What do you get if you cross a kangaroo with a skyscraper ?

A high jumper !

What do you get if you cross a road with a safari park ?

Double yellow lions !

What do you get if you cross an artist with a policeman ?

A brush with the law !

What do you get if you cross an overweight golfer and a pair of very tight trousers ?

A hole in one !

What do you get if you cross a plumber with
a field of cow pats ?

The poohed piper !

What do you get if you cross an elephant
and a bottle of whisky ?

Trunk and disorderly !

What do you get if you cross a flock
of sheep and a radiator ?

Central bleating !

CROSSES

What do you get if you cross a skunk
and a pair of tennis rackets?

Ping pong!

What do you get if you cross a pudding
and a cow pat?

A Smelly Jelly!

What do you get if you cross a pig and
a box of itching powder?

Pork scratching!

What do you get if you cross a bear with a freezer ?

A teddy brrrrrr !

What do you get if you cross a computer with a vampire ?

Something new fangled !

What do you get if you cross a tin opener, a vampire and a cricket team ?

An opening bat !

What do you get if you cross a cow with a grass cutter ?

A lawn mooer !

What do you get if you cross an
ice cream with a dog ?

Frost-bite !

What do you get if you cross a helicopter
with a cornish pasty ?

Something pie in the sky !

What do you get if you cross a pair of dogs with a
hairdresser ?

A shampoodle and setter !

What do you get if you cross a shoulder
bag with a Mallard ?

A ducksack !

What do you get if you cross a dinosaur with a dog ?

Tyrannosaurus Rex !

What do you get if you cross a football team with a
bunch of crazy jokers ?

Mad jester United !

What do you get if you cross a Viking
and a detective ?

Inspector Norse!

What do you get if you cross a large computer and a
beefburger ?

A Big Mac !

What do you get if
you cross an overheating
large computer with a
beefburger ?

A Big Mac and fries !

What do you get if
you cross a hat factory
and a field of cows ?

A pat on the head !

What do you get if you cross a mouse
and a bottle of olive oil?

A squeak that oils itself!

What do you get if you cross a jogger
with an apple pie?

Puff pastry!

What do you get if you cross a detective with a cat?

A peeping Tom!

What do you get if you cross a TV programme
and a load of sheep ?

A flock-U-mentary !

What do you get if you cross a footballer
and a mythical creature ?

A centaur forward !

What do you get if you cross an actress and a glove
puppet ?

Sooty and Streep !

What do you get if you cross a pasty
and a scary film ?

A Cornish nasty !

What do you get if you cross a pig
and a part in a film ?

A ham roll !

What do you get if you cross a sports
reporter with a vegetable ?

A common tater !

What do you get if you cross a wireless with a hairdresser ?

Radio waves !

What do you get if you cross a hairdresser and a bucket of cement ?

Permanenl waves !

What do you get if you cross a toadstool and a full suitcase ?

Not mushroom for your holiday clothes !

What do you get if you cross a dog with a vampire ?

A were - woof !

What do you get if you cross a bike and a rose ?

Bicycle petals !

What do you get if you cross an alligator
and King Midas ?

A croc of gold !

CROSSES

What do you get if you cross a tortoise and a storm ?

An 'I'm not in a hurry cane !'

What do you get if you cross a chicken with a pod ?

Chick peas !

What do you get if you cross a computer
with a potato ?

Micro chips !

What do you get if you cross a dog with a maze ?

A labyrinth !

What do you get if you cross a cow with a crystal ball ?

A message from the udder side !

What do you get if you cross a
crocodile with a camera ?

A snapshot !

What do you get if you cross a chicken
and an electricity socket ?

A battery hen !

What do you get if you cross a plank of wood
and a pencil ?

A drawing board !

What do you get if
you cross a dog
with a football game ?

Spot-The-Ball !

What do you get if
you cross a spider
with a computer ?

A web page !

What do you get if you cross a toilet with a
pop singer ?

Loo - Loo !

What do you get if you cross a frog
with a traffic warden ?

Toad away !

What do you get if you cross a flea
with some moon rock ?

A lunar - tick !

What do you get if you cross a vampire
and a circus entertainer ?

Something that goes straight for the juggler !

What do you get if you cross a snake
with a building site ?

A boa-constructor !

What do you get if you cross a parrot
with an alarm clock ?

Politics !

What do you get if you cross a bottle of
washing up liquid and a mouse ?

Bubble and squeak !

What do you get if you cross a mountain
and a baby ?

A cry for Alp !

What do you get if you cross a bunch
of flowers with some insects ?

Ants in your plants !

What do you get if you cross a bunch of flowers with a burgler ?

Robbery with violets !

What do you get if you cross a cow and a goat ?

Butter from a butter !

What do you get if you cross a pair of hiking boots and a parrot ?

A walkie-talkie !

What do you get if
you cross a
pen with
Napoleon's feet?

A footnote
in history!

What do you get if
you cross a skunk
and a pair of
rubber boots?

Smelly wellies!

What do you get if you cross a ghost
and an Italian restaurant?

Spookhetti!

What do you get if you cross a cow
with an out of date map?

Udderly lost!

What do you get if you cross a TV soap
and a rabbit colony ?

Burrow Nation Street !

What do you get if you cross a pelican and a zebra ?

Across the road safely !

What do you get if
you cross a bee
and a coach ?

A Buzzzz !

What do you get if
you cross a
monster and a
chicken ?

Free strange eggs !

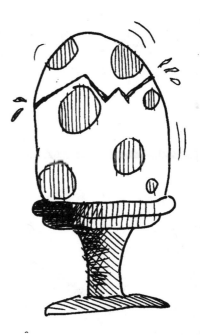

What do you get if you cross a fish
and bad breath ?

Halibut - osis !

What do you get if you cross a
compass and a shellfish ?

A guided mussel !

What do you get if you cross a school
with a computer supplier ?

Floppy Desks !

CROSSES

What do you get if you cross a baby with soldiers ?

Infantry !

What do you get if you cross a very bent piece
of wood with a spaceship ?

Warp factor 7 !

What do you get if you cross a hairdresser,
a storyteller and a young horse ?

A pony tail !

What do you get if
you cross a
motorcycle and
a funny story ?

A Yamaha ha ha ha !

What do you get if you cross a leopard
and a bunch of flowers ?

A beauty spot !

What do you get if you cross a biscuit with a car tyre ?

Crumbs !

What do you get if you cross a rabbit
and an aeroplane ?

The hare force !

What do you get if you cross a
Welshman with a problem ?

A Dai - lemma !

What do you get if you cross a pub and a steelworks ?

An iron bar !

What do you get if you cross a cow
and a jogging machine ?

A milk shake !

What do you get if you cross a book
and a pound of fat ?

Lard of the Rings !

What do you get if you cross a
newsreader and a toad ?

A croaksman !

What do you get if you cross a
ghost and a newsreader ?

A Spooksman !

What do you get if you cross a
suitcase with a filbert ?

A nut case !

CROSSES

What do you get if you cross a donkey
and Christmas ?

Muletide greetings !

What do you get if you cross the devil
and an anagram ?

Santa !

What do you get if you cross a Shakespeare
play and 3 eggs ?

Omelette !

What do you get if you cross a Shakespeare play
and a pig ?

A Ham omelette !

What do you get if you cross a Shakespeare
play and a vampire ?

Bat breath !

What do you get if you cross an
Eskimo and an ex-boyfriend ?

The cold shoulder !

What do you get if you cross a penguin and an elk ?

Chocolate moose !

CROSSES

What do you get if you cross a chemical and a bicycle?

Bike carbonate of soda!

What do you get if you cross a skeleton,
a feather and a joke book?

Rib ticklers!

What do you get if you cross a
skeleton and a garden spade?

Skullduggery!

What do you get if you cross a skeleton and a dog?

An animal that buries itself!

What do you get if you cross a
skeleton and a tumble drier?

Bone dry clothes!

What do you get if you cross
a fish and a Yamaha?

A motor pike!

What do you get if you cross a radio music presenter with Match of the Day ?

D D D D D D D D D D D D D D J !

What do you get if you cross teeth with candy ?

Dental floss !

What do you get if you cross
a Spice Girl with a pudding ?

A Jelly Baby !

What do you get if you go on a blind date
wearing football boots ?

Stud up !

What do you get if you cross a
mad man and a bakery ?

Doughnuts !

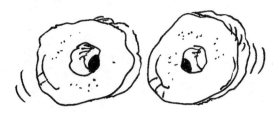

What do you get if you cross a
vampire and a bowl of soup ?

Scream of Tomato !

What do you get if you cross a pig and a laundry ?

Hogwash !

CROSSES

What do you get if you cross a cake and a disco ?

Abundance !

What do you get if you cross a bad tempered witch doctor, a fizzy drink and your dad ?

A bottle of pop !

What do you get if you cross a dog and a film studio ?

Collie - wood !

What do you get if you cross an insect and a dance ?

A cricket ball !

What do you get if you cross a giant ape and a self defence class ?

Kong - Fu !

What do you get if you cross a jet engine
and a tennis racket ?

A Tennis Rocket !

What do you get if you cross a sheep with a holiday
resort ?

The Baaahaaamaaas !

What do you get if you cross a sheep and a vampire ?

A were - wool !

What do you get if you cross a King and a boat ?

King Canoe !

What do you get if you cross a herb and
Doctor Who ?

A thyme machine !

What do you get if you cross two sailors and a
bottle of HP ?

Tartare Sauce !

What do you get if you cross a telephone
and a marriage bureau ?

A Wedding Ring !

What do you get if you cross a doctor's
surgery and a mountain range ?

Peak Practice !

What do you get if you cross a pig and an
emergency vehicle ?

A Hambulance !

What do you get if you cross a joke book
and a snowstorm ?

Corn Flakes !

What do you get if you cross a pig
and a telephone ?

A lot of crackling on the line !

What do you get if you cross a
vampire and a plumber ?

A drain in the neck !

What do you get if you cross an
Italian landmark and a ghost ?

The screaming tower of Pisa !

What do you get if you cross a
vampire with a mummy ?

Something you wouldn't want to unwrap !

What do you get if you cross a carrier pigeon
with a woodpecker?

A bird that knocks before delivering a message !

What do you get if you cross a frog
and a secret agent ?

A croak and dagger story !

What do you get if you cross a jellyfish
and an aircraft ?

A jelly copter !

What do you get if you cross a naked woman
and the bottom of the ocean ?

A deep sea Lady Godiva !

What do you get if you cross a singer and
a tall ladder ?

Someone who can easily get the high notes !

What do you get if you cross a
student and an alien ?

Something from another universe - ity !

What do you get if you cross an
alien and a hot drink ?

Gravi - tea !

What do you get if you cross a
mummy and a spaceship ?

Tutankha - moon !

What do you get if you cross a
gorilla and a prisoner ?

A Kong - vict !

HOSPITAL

Doctor, doctor...
my son is turning into a cricket bat !

Hmm ! Well, this has got me stumped !

Why did the angry doctor have to retire ?

Because he had lost all his patients !

Doctor, doctor...
I think I've got an inferiority complex !

No you haven't - you really are inferior !

Ah. Mr Smith, have your eyes ever been checked ?

No doctor, they've always been blue !

Doctor, doctor...
There's a man to see you with a wooden leg called Jenkins.

What's his other leg called ?

Doctor, doctor...
I think I'm turning into a wasp !

Hmm , give me a buzz if things get really bad !

Doctor, doctor...
I've just been stung by a wasp !

Did you put anything on it ?

No, he seemed to enjoy it just as it was !

BEE OINTMENT

Doctor, doctor...
I've got an itchy spotty patch on my nose,
should I put cream on it ?

Now, now, let's not do anything rash !

Doctor, doctor...
I've not stopped laughing since my operation !

Well, I told you the surgeon would have you in stitches !

Doctor, doctor...
I've got pigeon toes !

Don't worry we'll find a suitable tweetment for you...
but for now just put this birdseed in your shoes !

Doctor, doctor...
My belly is so big I'm embarrassed by it !

Have you tried to diet ?

Yes, but whatever colour I use it still sticks out !

Doctor's Bookcase...

TRAINING TO BE A SURGEON

by

I. CUTTEM - OPEN

Doctor, doctor...
I feel like a twenty pound note !

Go shopping, the change will do you good !

Doctor, doctor...
I can't stop shoplifting !

Try taking two of these pills every morning,
and if that doesn't work bring me
a CD player next week !

Doctor, doctor...
Did you hear about the appendix who
went out and bought a new suit -
because he heard that the doctor was
going to take him out !

Doctor, doctor...
Which king was also a doctor ?

William the corn curer !

Doctor, doctor...
Is it true that you can get pills to improve your memory ?

Of course you can, how many would you like ?

How many what ?

Doctor, doctor...
Which kings needed medical attention ?

**Charles the sick
and
Henry the ache !**

Doctor, doctor...
I feel as sick as a dog !

I'll make an appointment for you to see a vet !

Doctor, doctor...
Thank you for coming - I'm at death's door !

Don't worry, I'll pull you through !

Doctor, doctor...
What can I do to help me get to sleep ?

Have you tried counting sheep ?

Yes, but then I have to wake up to drive home again !

Doctor, doctor...
I've got a terrible cough!

Well you should practice more!

Doctor, doctor...
After the operation on my hand
will I be able to play the piano?
Of course you will Mr Smith!

**Great - because I never
could before!**

Doctor, doctor...
my son is turning into a
cricket bat!

**Hmm! Well, this has got me
stumped!**

Doctor, doctor...
I think I'm turning into a fish!

Well, just hop up on to the scales!

Doctor, doctor...
I feel like a goat!

Really - and how are the kids?

Doctor, doctor...
I think I'm turning into a bridge!

Really - what's come over you?

Doctor, doctor...
Why did the chemist tell everyone to be quiet?

Because she didn't want to wake the sleeping pills!

Doctor, doctor...
These tablets you gave me last week seem
to get smaller every day ?!

Yes, they're slimming pills !

Doctor, doctor...
I think I'm turning into a toad !

Don't worry, we can do an hoperation
for that these days !

Doctor, doctor...
Can you put me in touch with the local plastic surgeon ?

I'm afraid not, he sat too close to the
radiator last night and melted !
Doctor, doctor...
I have a fish hook stuck in the side of my mouth !

I thought you were waiting to see me
with baited breath !

Doctor, doctor...
I've just been stung by a giant wasp !

I'll give you some cream to put on it !

Don't be daft - it'll be miles away by now !

Doctor, doctor...
My new job at the laundry is very tiring !

I thought you looked washed out !

Ah. Mr Blenkinsop. Did you drink the medicine
I gave you after your bath ?

**No, Doctor, I couldn't even drink all the bath
let alone the medicine !**

Doctor, doctor...
I get a lot of headaches from my wooden leg.

Why is that ?

**Because my wife keeps hitting me
over the head with it !**

Doctor, doctor...
I think I have a split personality !

I'd better give you a second opinion then !

Doctor, doctor...
I got trampled by a load of cows !

So I herd !

Doctor, doctor...
I keep imagining I,m a sunken ship and it's
really got me worried !

Sounds to me like you're a nervous wreck !

Doctor, doctor...
My snoring wakes me up every night !

Try sleeping in another bedroom, then you
won't be able to hear it !

Doctor, doctor...
I feel quite like my old self again !

Oh Dear, I better put you back on the tablets then !

Doctor, doctor...
I think I have acute appendicitis !

Yes, it is rather nice isn't it !
Doctor, doctor...

My hair is falling out - can you give me something to keep it in ?

Here's a paper bag ?!

Doctor, doctor...
What can you give me for my kidneys ?

How about a pound of onions ?!

Doctor, doctor...
I've fractured my elbow bone !

Humerus ?

Well, I don't think it's particularly funny !
Doctor, doctor...

Is this disease contagious ?

Not at all !

Then why are you standing out on the window ledge ?!

Doctor, doctor...
You don't really think I'm turning into a
grandfather clock do you ?

No, I was just winding you up !

Doctor, doctor...
I keep thinking I'm a big bar of chocolate !

Come and sit here, and don't worry, I won't bite – I'm
just a big old pussycat really !

SCHOOL

hat do you call someone who greets you
at the school door every morning?

Matt!

Teacher - Blenkinsop - Give me a sentence with the word detention in it !

Blenkinsop - I had to leave the horror film before it had finished, because I couldn't stand detention !

Head - Why haven't you been in school for the last two weeks ?

Pupil - It's not my fault - whenever I get to the road outside the school I'm never allowed to cross!

Head - Why aren't you allowed to cross ?

Pupil - Because there is a man with a sign saying 'STOP CHILDREN CROSSING'!

Fred – YUK! These school dinners taste of soap!

Freda – Well, at least you know the kitchens are clean!

Where would you find giant snails...?

...at the end of giant's fingers !

5 GOOD REASONS TO GO TO SCHOOL...

1   Even school dinners are better than my dad's.

2   The heating goes off at home at 9 o'clock.

3   You learn to be independent - by doing as you're told!

4   The video shop doesn't open 'til 4 o'clock!

5   You learn what life will be like when you are old and grumpy - by watching the teachers at coffee break.

Blenkinsop - Sir, my parents want me to tell you that they were really pleased with my last report.

Teacher - But I said you were a **complete** idiot ?

Blenkinsop - But it's the first time anyone in our family has been really good at something!

Head - What do think about in the school holidays ?

Pupil - I never think about schoolwork !

Head - Not really much of a change for you then ?

Head - Mr Snurge, why have you put the school orchestra into the school freezer ?

Mr Snurge - They said they wanted to play some music that was a little more cool !?

For tonight's homework I want you to write an essay on a goldfish.

I can't do that Sir !

Why on earth not ?

I don't have any waterproof ink !

I'm not really interested in maths - I just go along to the lesson to make up the numbers!

Teacher - *Name a bird that doesn't build its own nest.*

Blenkinsop - The Cuckoo.

Teacher - That' right - how on earth did you know that ?

Blenkinsop - Everyone knows that Cuckoos live in clocks!

DID YOU HEAR ABOUT...

The P.E. teacher who used to run round the exam room in the hope of jogging pupils memories ?

The maths teacher and the art teacher who used to go out together painting by numbers ?

The craft teacher who used to have the class in stitches ?

The science teacher who was scared of little glass dishes - he was petrified ?

The cookery teacher who thought Hamlet was an omelette served with bacon ?

Why did the school canteen hire a dentist ?

To make more filling meals !

I banged my head on my locker door this morning !

Have you seen the school nurse ?

No, just stars !

Head - Why were you sent out of the
tennis class today ?

Pupil - For making a racket !

What exams do farmyard animals take ?

Hay levels !

Teacher - Blenkinsop , If five cats were on a bus and one get off, how many would be left ?

Blenkinsop - None, sir !

Teacher - How do you get that answer ?

Blenkinsop - Because the other 4 were copycats !

Teacher - Who can tell me which sea creature eats its prey two at a time ?

Pupil - Noah's Shark !

Which of Shakespeare's plays was
about a bacon factory ?

Hamlet !

What's the difference between a
bird watcher and a teenager ?

One gets a hide and spots, the other
gets a spot and hides !

Why is Frankenstein's
monster rubbish at school ?

He hasn't got the brains he
was born with !

Teacher - Smith, what were
people wearing during the
Great Fire of London ?

Smith - Blazers, smoking
jackets and hose ?

What is a good pet for small children ?

A Rattlesnake ??

Why were ancient sailing ships more eco-friendly ?

**Because they could go for hundreds
of miles to the galleon !**

Teacher - Smith, I do wish you would pay a
little attention !

Smith - I'm paying as little as I can, sir !

Teacher - Did you find the exam questions easy?

Pupil - Oh, yes I found the question all right, it's the answers I couldn't find!

Why does our robot games teacher never get sick?

Because he has a cast iron constitution!

Teacher - Mary, why was no-one able to play cards on Noah's Ark?

Mary - Because Noah stood on the deck!

Teacher - John, name me a famous religious warrior!

John - Attilla the Nun?

Teacher – Smith, where are you from ?

Smith – London.

Teacher – Which part ?

Smith – All of me !

Teacher – Did you know that most accidents happen in the kitchen ?

Pupil – Yes, but we still have to eat them !

Teacher – Who was Thor ?

Pupil – The God who kept Thcratching hith thpot !

How do you cure lockjaw ?

Swallow a key ?

Teacher – If you had to multiply 1345 by 678
what would you get ?

Sarah – the wrong answer !

John - Dad, have we got a ladder ?

Dad - What do you need that for ?

John - For homework I have to write
an essay on an elephant !

English Teacher - Did anyone help you
write this poem Carol ?

Carol - No Miss.

English Teacher - Well, I'm delighted to meet
you at last Mr Shakespeare !

Teacher - Sid - what is a goblet ?

Sid - A baby turkey ?

H NEW BOOKS IN THE GEOGRAPHY LIBRARY H

RICE GROWING IN CHINA by Paddy Fields

AFRICAN SAFARI by Rhoda Lion

EXPLORING SPACE by Honor Rocket

THE FROZEN WASTES by S. Keemo

CLIMBING EVEREST by Percy Veerance

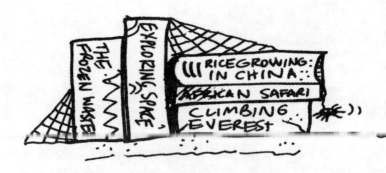

Teacher - Steven, name an ancient musical instrument.

Steven - An Anglo - saxophone ?

Teacher - Jim, what is the largest species of mouse in the World ?

Jim - The Hippo pota - mouse !

Teacher - Sarah, what evidence is there that smoking is harmful to the health ?

Sarah - Well, just look what happened to all the dragons !

ANIMAL SCHOOL REPORTS...

Cheetah - A nice enough boy, but not to be trusted.

Leopard - Has missed a lot of classes
this year due to spots

Hyena - Seems to think that everything is a joke

Stick Insect - Never been the same since the elephant
mistook him for a pencil !

Why did the boy throw his wristwatch out
of the window in the history exam ?

He wanted to make time fly !

Teacher – Smith, why is the handwriting in your homework book exactly the same as Blenkinsops ?

Smith – I borrowed his pen ?!

Teacher – Why were you late for school today Carol ?

Carol – I got a flat tyre on my bicycle !

Teacher – Did you run over some broken glass ?

Carol – No, sir, there was a fork in the road !

Head – I want you all to be aware of the importance of punctuality !

Blenkinsop – Well, I should be alright, I get good marks in English !

Teacher - Steven, what's a computer byte ?

Steven - I didn't even know they had teeth !

Head - Have you any idea how many teachers work at this school ?

Pupil - About a quarter of them it seems to me !

Teacher - Why were you late this morning Veronica ?

Veronica - I squeezed the toothpaste too hard, and it took me half an hour to get it all back into the tube again !

You have a photographic memory Blenkinsop,
it's a shame that nothing ever develops !

Teacher - jarvis, tell me a sentence with the
word counterfeit in it.

Jarvis - I wasn't sure if she was a centipede or
a millipede so I had to count her feet !

Computer Teacher - Smith, give me an
example of software.

Smith - A floppy hat ?

Teacher - How would you stop a cockerel waking you at 5 a.m. ?

Pupil - Eat him for supper before you go to bed !

The Deputy Head is a funny chap,
who creeps from class to class,
he has a face that could curdle cream
and a voice like broken glass !

Teacher - Blenkinsop, How would you discover what life in Ancient Egypt was really like ?

Blenkinsop - I'd ask my Mummy !

What's the difference between a school
and a headmaster's car?

One breaks up, the other breaks down!

Teacher - What's the difference between a
horse and an elephant?

Pupil - A horse doesn't look like an elephant!

A bottle of lemonade went to teacher training college
what subject was he going to teach?

Fizzical education!

A butterfly went to teacher training college -
what subject was she going to teach?

Moth - a - matics!

Teacher - Who discovered Pluto?

Pupil - Walt Disney?

Pupil - Ugh! There;'s a fly in my soup!

Kitchen assistant - Don't worry, the spider
on your bread will get it!

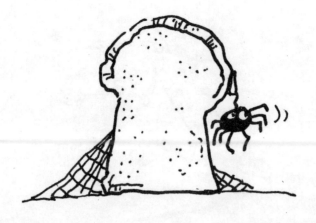

Blenkinsop , what do birds eat for their breakfast ?

Tweet - a - bix ?!

Did you hear about the music teacher who kept
forgetting her register !?

We love our school
We really do
We love our lessons
Teachers too!

We love the exams
and the tricky tests
We love the school dinners
and the P.E. vests !

But why do I sound
so cheerful today
Because we just started
the Summer holiday !!

Teacher - Have you been an idiot all your life ?

Pupil - No, not yet !

What do you call the German teacher who
goes to school on a motor bike ?

Helmut !

Why are teachers like doctors ?

Because they are both good at examinations !

When are skipping ropes like schoolchildren ?

When they are taught !

Why did the teacher leave his job ?

He was head hunted !

Blenkinsop, why are you looking in lost property?

My granny moved house last week and I can't remember where she lives now!

Surely you can remember what happened in 1066?

It's alright for you, sir, you were there!

Sarah. I think your father has been helping you with your homework !

No, Miss, he did it all by himself !

Today we are going to look for the lowest common denominator...

Haven't they found that yet, my dad says they were looking for that when he was at school !

Blenkinsop - you deserve a hundred lines for this homework !

Ah, but it wouldn't be fair on the rest of the class if I always got what I deserved would it, sir !

Parent – Do you think my son will make a good Arctic explorer ?

Teacher – I would think so, most of his marks are below zero !

Teacher – You should have been here at 9 o'clock this morning !

Parent – Why, did something happen ?

Please don't talk while you are doing your exam !

It's alright, miss, we're not doing the exam – just talking !

Science teacher - Name two liquids that don't freeze...

Mary - Coffee and tea !

History teacher - Who shot King Harold ?

Blenkinsop - My mum told me never to tell tales !

Geography teacher - Where is Hadrian's wall ?

Blenkinsop - Where he left it !

Why are maths teachers no good at gardening ?

Because everything they plant grows square roots !

Did you hear about the maths teacher whose mistakes started to multiply ?

They took him away in the end !

Did you hear about the two history teachers who met on television ?

They were on Blind Date !

Did you hear about the stupid P.E. teacher ?

He was a physical jerk !

Susie, How do you make a milk shake?

Take it to a scary film, Miss!

Blenkinsop, do you understand how important punctuation is?

Yes, Miss, I always make sure I get to school on time!

Mark, how did Moses cut the sea in half ?

With a sea-saw ?

Wendy, when do you like school the best ?

During the school holidays, Sir !

What do skeleton teachers say at the start of the lesson ?

As there is nobody here we can start !

Brian, what is water ?

A colourless liquid which turns black when
I put my hands in it !

You, boy, which part of a fish weighs the most ?

The scales, sir ?

What do Atilla the Hun and Winnie the
Pooh have in common ?

The !

Smith, name me someone who has been round the globe?

Terminator, Miss!

Who on earth is Terminator?

My goldfish!!

Watson, shouldn't you wash your hands before you start your piano lesson?

No, Miss, I only play on the black notes!

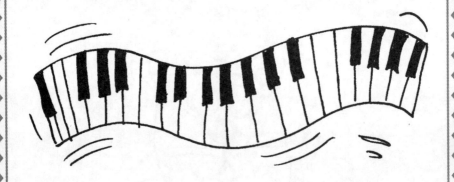

Carol, what is the difference between a policeman and a soldier?

You can't dip a policeman into your boiled egg, Sir!

Now, Roger, if a half filled barrel of beer fell on someone, how badly hurt would they be?

Not at all if it was light ale, Miss !?

Why are you putting in those ear plugs?

I've got to teach form 4B tennis, and they always make such a racket !

Now, can anyone tell me what Egyptian Kings were buried with?

Yes, Miss, they were buried with their Nammaforrs !

What is a Nammaforr ?

Knocking nails in !

Blenkinsop, how can you prove that the
Earth is round ?

I didn't say it was, Sir !

What do you call a
teacher swearing ?

A Sir - Cuss !

What did you think
of your first day at
school Joe ?

First ?! You mean I
have to go back again !

What is the difference between frogspawn and school pudding?

Frogspawn was once warm!

How can you tell if a teacher is in a good mood?

Let me know if you ever find out!

Why are you always late for school?

It's not my fault, you always ring the bell before I get here!

Why did the teacher make you take the chicken out of the classroom?

He said he didn't want anyone to hear fowl language in his lesson!

Howard, which is the largest sea ?

The Galax-sea !

What is a bunsen burner used for ?

Setting fire to bunsens, Miss ?

Sir, can we do some work on the Iron Age today ?

Well, I'm not certain, I'm a bit rusty on
that period of history !

Smith, How would you hire a horse ?

Put a brick under each leg ?

Why did Cyclops
have to retire
from teaching ?

He only had
one pupil !

Why is your
homework late,
Bloggs ?

Sorry, Miss,
my Dad is a
slow writer !

Did you hear about the teacher who went
to a mind reader ?

She gave him his money back !

Blenkinsop, how do you get rid of varnish ?

Just take out the 'R', Miss !

Smith, where do fish sleep ?

On a waterbed ?

Harry, what does it mean if I say
'Guten Morgen Herr Dresser' ?

It means you've gone for a haircut !

Sally, what musical instrument do Spanish fishermen play ?

Cast - a - nets ?

Bill, which is heavier, a full moon or a half moon ?

A half moon, because a full moon is lighter !

Mary, how did you find the questions in your English exam ?

Oh, I found the questions easily enough, it's the answers I couldn't find !

Geoff, why are you eating with a knife ?

Because my fork leaks !

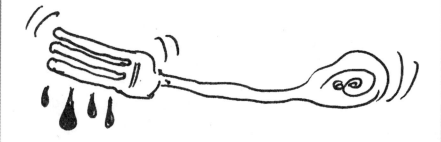

Who invented fractions ?

Henry the eighth !

Ten cats were at the cinema; one walked out,
how many were left ?

None - they were all copycats !

Wally, what is a dumb waiter ?

Someone who gets all the orders mixed up, Sir ??

Sue, describe crude oil for me !

Well, Sir, it is black and sticky and it floats on the surface
of water shouting 'knickers' !

Joe, how many seconds are there in a year?

Twelve, Miss, January 2nd, February 2nd,
March 2nd, April 2nd....

Flora, what is the most important
tool we use in mathematics?

Multi - pliers!

Fred, where do most spiders live?

Crawley!

Did you hear about the two history teachers
who got married ?

They liked to sit at home talking about old times !

Where did the metalwork teacher meet his wife ?

In a bar !

What happened after the wheel was first invented ?

It caused a revolution !

Robert, why do doctors and nurses wear
masks in the operating theatre ?

So no-one will know who did it if they make a mistake !

How do archaeologists get into locked tombs ?

Do they use a skeleton key, Miss ?

I've just got a place in the school football team - the games teacher says I'm the main drawback !

Steven, why did Henry the eighth have so many wives ?

He liked to chop and change, Miss ?

Why did the very first chips not taste very nice ?

Because they were fried in ancient Greece !

Sarah, where would you find a gorilla?

In a kitchen?

Jane, what do you know about the Dead Sea?

I didn't even know it had been poorly, Sir!

William, what is a fungi?

A mushroom that likes having a good time?

'John can't come to school today,
because he has a cold.'

'Who am I speaking to?'

'My father.'

Harry, spell 'mouse' trap...

C. A. T. !

Where do vampire teachers train ?

Teacher Draining College !

Billy, what is a wombat ?

It's what you use to play Wom, Miss !

Carol, can you give me a sentence with deliberate in it ?

'My dad bought a new settee and tomorrow they are going to deliberate to our house !'

What do you call the teacher who
organises all the exams ?

Mark !

Blenkinsop, I do wish you would pay a little attention !

I'm paying as little as I can, Sir !

Fred, how do fleas get from one animal to another ?

They itch hike !

Gloria, did you write this poem all by yourself?

Yes, Miss!

Well, well, and I thought Shakespeare was a man!

John, what is the longest word in the English dictionary?

Elastic!

How do you work that out?

It stretches!

James, give me a sentence with the word fascinate in it!

Fatty Perkins' coat has ten buttons, but he can only fascinate of them!

Howard, If I had 12 sausages in one hand, and 15 sausages in the other, how many sausages would I have altogether ?

No idea, Miss, I'm a vegetarian !

Freda will make a good astronomer when she leaves school, as she is very good at staring into space for hours on end !

What makes you think that my son, Martin, is always playing truant ?

Martin ? There's no Martin in this school !

What do you call a man who keeps on talking when no-one is listening ?

Sir !

I hope I don't catch you cheating in the maths exam !

So do I, Miss !

Fred, what food do giraffe's eat ?

Neck - tarines !

Mary, why have you brought that fish into school ?

Because we will be practising scales in the music lesson !

Jim, why did Robin Hood steal from the rich ?

Because the poor didn't have anything worth stealing !

Florence, where were most English Kings
and Queens crowned?

On the head ?!

Robert, why have you been suspended from school?

Because the boy next to me was smoking!

But if he was smoking, why were you suspended ??

Because I was the one who set fire to him!

Ian, when was the Forth bridge constructed?

After the first three had all fallen down?

Graham, what is a crane?

A bird that can lift really heavy weights ?!

Philip, why do you always have two plates
of food for school dinner?

It's important to have a balanced diet, Miss!

Mandy, do you have to come to school chewing gum?

No, Sir, I can stay at home and chew it if your prefer!

Did you hear about the maths teacher
who was taken away?

Where were traitors beheaded?

Just above the shoulders!

Graham, what are net profits?

What fishermen have left after paying the crew?

William, how do you make a Mexican chilli?

Take him to the South Pole, Miss!

BRRR   BRRR

Mum: Do you say a little prayer before you eat your school dinner?

Son: Good heavens no - the food isn't that bad!

George, you have had a very undistinguished career at this school - have you ever been first in anything?

Only the lunch queue, Miss!

Why is the school cheese on toast hairy?

Because the cook dropped it on the floor then wiped it on her jumper!

THE COLOSSAL KIDS' JOKE BOOK

How can bats fly without bumping into anything?

They use their wing mirrors!

Sarah, give me a sentence with the word illegal in it!

My dad took me to the bird hospital the other day and
we saw a sick sparrow and an illegal!

William, how fast does light travel?

I don't know, Sir, it's already arrived
by the time I wake up!

What do you give a sick bird ?

Tweetment !

How many maths teachers can you get in an empty Mini ?

Just one - after that it isn't empty any more !

Miriam, what is the hottest planet in our solar system ?

Mer - Curry !

Time to get up and go to school !

I don't want to go! Everyone hates me and I get bullied !

But you have to go - you're the headteacher !

Fred: Our teacher left last week and we all chipped in
to buy her a bottle of toilet water. It cost £15 !

Jane: Wow, I would have given you a whole bucket
of water from my toilet for 50 pence !

Your teacher says you're disgusting and
not fit to live with pigs !

What did you say ?

I stuck up for you, I said yes you are !

Teacher: Millie, why do you say that Moses wore a wig ?

Millie: Because sometimes he was seen with Aaron, and
sometimes without !

Pupil - Those eggs look a bit past their best !

School Cook - Don't blame me, I only laid the tables !

What do you call an American cartoonist ?

Yankee Doodle !

Blenkinsop, you could be in the school football team, if it weren't for two things !

What are they, Sir ?

Your feet !

BLENKINSOP'S FEET !

In South America, cowboys chase cattle
on horseback !

WOW ! I didn't know cows could ride at all !

Who was the fastest runner of all time ?

Adam, because he was first in the human race !

My dad baked some cakes, and said I have to
give one to my teacher !

Gee ! I never realised just how much he
must hate your teacher !

Blenkinsop - Why do birds fly South in the Winter ?

Because it is too far to walk !

What is a snake's favourite subject ?

Hissss-tory !

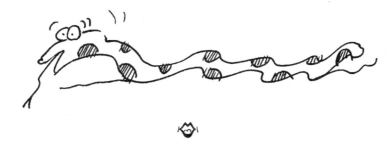

I told my dad I needed an encyclopedia for school !

What did he say ?

He said I could go on the bus like everyone else !

Head - You start on £20,000 a year, but go on to £24,000 after the first year.

Teacher - Oh ! Well, I'll come back in a year and start work then !

What does an elf do after school ?

Gnome work !

You have to be a really good whistler to
use the school toilets here !

Why is that ?

The locks are all broken !

If I cut a potato in two, I have two halves.
If I cut a potato in four, I have four quarters.
What do I have if I cut a potato in sixteen ?

Chips !

How did knights make chain mail?

From steel wool?

Why did the flea get thrown out of school?

He just wasn't up to scratch!

Why was the glow worm sad?

Because her children weren't very bright!

In this examination you will be allowed
15 minutes for each question !

Crikey, they sound like long questions !

What did the music teacher need a ladder for ?

Reaching the top notes !

Your son will be a good printer's assistant !

What makes you say that ?

He's exactly the right type !

Did you have any problems with your
French on your school trip to Paris ?

No, but the French certainly did !

Terry - how do you join the Police Force ?

Handcuff them together ?

John, name one use of Beech wood !

Making deck chairs ?

What is easy to get into, but
difficult to get out of ?

Trouble !

My mum says the school beef pie is good for you
because it is full of iron !

That explains why it's so tough then !

What was the blackbird doing in the school library ?

Looking for bookworms !

Mary, What do you think a pair of
crocodile shoes would cost ?

That would depend on the size of your
crocodile's feet Miss !

Fred, I told you to write 100 lines because your
handwriting is so bad, but you have only done 75 !

Sorry Miss, but my maths is just as
bad as my handwriting !

Jim, what is 'won't' short for ?

Will not, Miss !

Very good. What is 'don't' short for ?

Er...Donut Miss ?

Harry, how would you fix a short circuit ?

Add some more wire to make it longer, Sir ?

Where do dim witches go ?

Spelling classes !

Well, Geoff, did you get a good position in the maths test yesterday ?

Yes, Sir, I was in front of a radiator, and next to the smartest person in the class !

What is the most important letter to a stick insect ?

The letter 'T' - without it he would be a sick insect !

Do you know a boy called Jim Wibley ?

Yes, he sleeps next to me in Geography !

Michael can you name two inventions that have helped mankind to get up in the world ?

... Yes, Miss, the stepladder and the alarm clock !

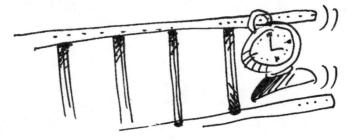

What do you call it when the Headteacher dosen't tell the truth about nits in his hair ?

Head Lice !

How many teachers work at your new school Samantha ?

About half of them !

Why was the teacher's head eleven inches long ?

Because if it was twelve inches it would be a foot !

What was Richard the Third's middle name ?

The !

You shouldn't play those notes on the piano !

Why not ?

You'll get into treble if you do !

Caroline, how many days of the week start
with the letter 'T' ?

Four: Tuesday,
Thursday,
Today and
Tomorrow !

The School Notice Board

Violin for sale - really cheap - no strings attached !

Dog free to good home - eats anything.
Loves children !

Why did the school orchestra have such
awful manners ?

Because it didn't know how to conduct itself !

What comes out of a teacher's wallet
at 100 miles an hour ?

Stirling Moth !

Table for sale, by Mr Wibley
with wooden legs !

On the school field trip a crab bit my toe !

Which one ?

I don't know, all crabs look the same to me !

ALIENS

What should you do with a green alien?

Wait until it's ripe!

What do you call an alien with two heads ?

A two-headed alien !

What do aliens do with humans they find in space ships ?

Put them in the larder - they keep
tinned food for emergencies !

What should you do if you
find a green alien ?

Wait until it's ripe !

Why do aliens have seven fingers on each hand ?

Because otherwise they would have two empty fingers in each glove !

Where do aliens live ?

In green houses !

What lights do aliens switch on every Saturday ?

Satellites !

What game do aliens play to while away the hours in deep space ?

Moonopoly !

Where do alien children
go in the evenings ?

Rocket and Roll concerts !

What are wealthy aliens members of ?

The Jet Set !

Where do aliens go to study their GCSEs ?

High School (Very High School) !

Why do aliens never starve in space ?

Because they always know where to find a Mars, a
Galaxy and a Milky Way !

What do evil aliens eat for lunch ?

Beans on toast - (Human Beans on toast) !

Why are aliens good for the environment ?

Because they are green !

What do aliens have to do before they can drive a rocket at twice the speed of light in deep space ?

Reverse it out of the garage !

What do aliens call junk food?

Unidentified Frying Objects!

How do you know when
aliens are envious?

Easy - they turn green!

What sort of sweets to Martians eat?

Martian mallows!

Where do aliens go to study rocket science?

Mooniversity!

How do you know when an alien is homesick?

He just moons about all over the place!

What do you give a sick alien ?

Planetcetamol !

What do giant space monsters play to relax ?

Squash !

How do you contact someone who lives on Saturn ?

Give them a ring !

What is the quickest way to get an alien baby to sleep ?

Rocket !

ALIEN SCHOOL REPORT

Music — He loves the Planet Suite by Holst !

Chemistry — Blew off one of his heads making rocket fuel !

Martian — KLargin SCRung jlkfr TTTTugt KLMgg FRelOOmmMw~We TTrRaaakk !

Maths — Can count up to seventeen using the fingers on his left hand !

Space — Takes a bite out of the Milky Way every time he goes there on a school trip !

What do you call an alien girl band ?

The Space Girls !

What do you call a mad alien ?

A Lunar-tic !

What game do nasty aliens play with Earth space ships ?

Shuttlecocks !

What is the name of the planet inhabited by video recorders ?

Planet of the Tapes !

What ticket do you ask for to go there for a holiday ?

Return to the Planet of the Tapes !

Which side of a spaceship passes
closest to the planets ?

The Outside !

Why did the impressionist crash through the ceiling ?

He was taking off a rocket taking off !

What does an alien gardener do with his hedges ?

Eclipse them every Spring !

Why did the alien buy a pocket computer?

So he could work out how many pockets he has!

How can you tell if a computer is disgruntled?

It will have a chip on its shoulder!

How do you get directions in deep space?

Askeroid!

Where do aliens keep fish they capture
from other planets?

In a planetarium!

Why did the alien school have no computers?

Because someone ate all the apples!

What do evil aliens grind up to make a hot drink?

Coffee beings!

What do you call an alien who travels through space on a ketchup bottle ?

A flying saucer !

Why did the attendant turn space ships away from the lunar car park ?

It was a full moon !

How does a Martian know he's attractive ?

When bits of metal stick to him !

What do you call a space ship made from cow pats ?

A Pooh F O !

Where do alien space ship pilots go to learn how to fly in the darkness of outer space ?

Night school !

What do you call a sad space ship ?

An unidentified crying object !

What does the alien from planet X
use to smooth her nails ?

The X Files, of course !

Do space ships like this crash very often?

Only the once!

Why are alien gardeners so good?

Because they have green fingers!

What do alien children do on Halloween?

They go from door to door dressed as humans!

How do you know if there is an alien in your house ?

There will be a spaceship parked in the garden !

How do you communicate with aliens out in deep space ?

You have to shout really loudly !

How do you tell if an alien is embarrassed ?

They blush - and their cheeks go purple !

How do you catch a Venusian mega mouse ?

In a Venusian mega mouse-trap !

What do you give a sick alien ?

Paracetamoons !

Where do aliens do their shopping ?

In a greengrocers !

Why do some aliens make their space ships out of twisted planks of wood ?

So they can travel at warp speed !

Who is in love with the alien james Bond ?

Miss Mooneypenny !

Where do aliens go for holidays?

Lanzarocket!

What do aliens put on their cakes?

Mars - ipan!

Who is the aliens' favourite robot
cartoon character?

Tin - Tin!

Why was the robot rubbing its joints with a video ?

Because it was a video of Grease !

What is a robot's favourite chocolate ?

Whole Nut !

Where are parts for robots made ?

In Bolton, Knutsford and Leeds !

What do you give a robot who fancies a light snack ?

Some 60 watt bulbs !

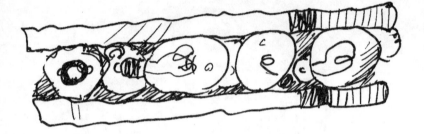

What did the teacher give the alien monster for lunch ?

Class 4B !

What sort of music do robots like best ?

Steel band music !

Who do robots vote for in a General Election ?

Tinny Blair !

How do you know when a robot
has been in your fridge ?

There are footprints in the butter !

How do you invite a robot to a party ?

Send round a tinvitation !

What firework do aliens like best ?

Rockets !

What did the robot say to the petrol pump ?

Take your finger out of your ear when I'm talking to you !

What is an alien's favourite TV programme ?

Blind date - it's the only way they can get a human girlfriend !

What do you call computer controlled sandpaper ?

Science Friction !

If you get lost in space - who should
you ask for directions ?

An alien hairdresser -
they know all the short cuts !

If an alien leaves his chewing gum orbiting
the Earth - what
do you call it ?

A Chew - F - O !

Your son will make an
excellent rocket pilot !

Why do you say that ?

He has nothing but
space between his ears !

Why do steel robots have so many friends ?

I suppose they must have magnetic personalities !

What do daleks drink ?

Exterminade !

What do aliens put on their toast ?

Mars - malade !

Where is the smelliest part of an alien spaceship ?

The Com - poooh - ter !

Why did the alien paint his spaceship
with sugar and vinegar ?

He wanted a sweet and sour saucer !

How do you tip an alien spaceship over ?

Rocket !

What did the greedy alien say when he
landed on a new planet ?

Take me to your larder !

What dance can you see in the night sky ?

The Moon Walk !

Why did the football manager want to get
in touch with the alien ?

Because he knew where all the shooting stars were !

What did the mummy robot say to her children ?

Look before you bleep !

Why was the young robot so happy ?

Because he didn't have a chip on his shoulder !

Where does the alien gardener keep his tools ?

In an astro - hut !

Where do Martians go to see a movie?

Cine - mars !

Knock, knock,
Who's there ?
Jupiter
Jupiter Who ?
Jupiter spaceship on my lawn ?

What is worse than finding a 12 legged Venusian
mega - maggot in your apple ?

Finding half a 12 legged Venusian
mega - maggot in your apple !

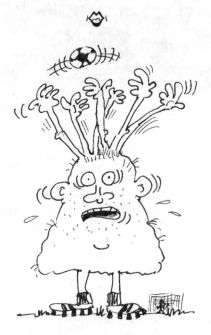

What did the referee book the alien for ?

Hand ball, Hand ball, Hand ball, Hand ball....

What do aliens use to go up and down ?

Stairs !

Where did they put the alien who stole a field full of rhubarb?

In Custardy!

What is green and very noisy?

An alien with a drum kit!

Who was the first man on the moon?

A Spaceman!

What did one rocket say to the other ?

I wish I could stop smoking !

I don't know what to buy my pal, the
space alien, for his birthday ?!

How about 5 pairs of slippers !

Why do astronauts never eat after take off ?

Because they have just had a big launch !

How often do you find toilets in space ?

Once in a loo moon !

why didn't the Martian have his
birthday party on the Moon ?

There was no atmosphere !

What is soft and sweet and fluffy
and comes from Mars ?

A Mars-mallow !

What do astronauts have in their packed lunch ?

Launcheon Meat !

What do astronauts wear when it's cold ?

Apollo neck jumpers !

How do you know that Saturn is married?

You can see the ring!

What game do bored Aliens play?

Astro noughts and crosses!

Why did the space monster cover his rocket
with tomato sauce?

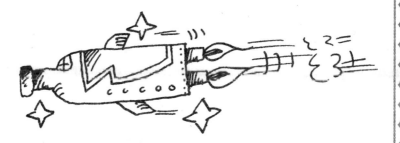

So the nasty aliens couldn't ketchup with him!

What do the aliens from the planet Skunkus ride in ?

Phew F O's !

When the alien picked up his brand new spaceship he was really pleased - he'd never had a **NEW F O** before !

What sort of spaceships do aliens from the planet Footwear use ?

Shoe F O's

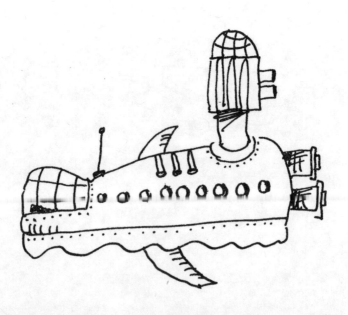

How did the space aliens go into the space ark ?

R 2 D 2 by R 2 D 2 !

Alien - Beware Earthling, I could eat your entire planet !

Blenkinsop - That's nothing, yesterday I ate an entire Galaxy !

What do you call a pub on Mars ?

A Mars bar !

Why did the spaceship land outside your bedroom ?

I must have left the landing light on !

What do you call a space creature that doesn't pass his space exams ?

A Fail-ien !

What do you get in an alien transport cafe ?

Unidentified frying objects !

What is the smallest space explorer called ?

A Mouse-tronaut !

What do space ramblers like to do ?

Go on Star Treks !

What do you never get if you cross a bug-eyed alien with a dog ?

Burgled !

What is the first thing an alien puts on
when he gets out of bed ?

His feet - ON - the floor !

Where do aliens keep their sandwiches ?

In a launch box !

Why are aliens good gardeners ?

They have green fingers !

Knock, knock...
Who's there ?
Jupiter.
Jupiter who ?

Jupiter space ship on my front lawn ?!

What goes in one year and out the other ?

A time machine !

If astronauts breathe oxygen during the day,
what do they breathe at night ?

Nitrogen !

Knock, knock...
Who's there ?
Saturn.
Saturn who ?

**Saturn front of this spaceship
waiting for take off time !**

What is the weakest part of space called ?

The Punyverse !

What robots are made from small planets ?

Aster - droids !

What do you call a vampire version of Star Trek ?

The Necks Generation !

Human –   Why have you got holes in your hand ?

Alien –   I have been using the computer.

Human –   But that's not dangerous !?

Alien –   Maybe not on Earth, but on my planet when
            we talk about computer bytes we mean
            something different !

Why do creatures from the planet THaaarRRgh wear slimy green braces ?

To hold their slimy green trousers up !

What do you call a glass robot ?

See through P O !

Why couldn't the moon eat any more supper ?

Because it was full !

What teddy bear story do robot children read at bedtime ?

Tinny - the - Pooh !

ALIENS

What does the alien hairdresser do when the shadow of the earth obscures the sun ?

Eclipse !

How do you get a baby alien to sleep ?

Rocket !

What did the grape say when the space monster trod on him ?

Nothing - he just let out a little whine !

What do you call a noisy space ship ?

A space racket !

What do space aliens watch on TV ?

Countdown !

Why is the letter V like a space monster ?

Because it comes after you !

What do you call the planet that is inhabited
solely by impressionists ?

Planet of the apes !

Which part of a space suit is German ?

The Helmut !

ALIENS

Which Egyptian King was named after a planet ?

Tutankhamoon !

Why are alien kitchens always such a mess ?

Because of all the flying sauces !

What did the tree alien say when he landed on Earth ?

Take me to your Cedar !

What would you do if you saw a spaceman ?

Park in it, man !

Why did the alien buy a twisted spaceship ?

He wanted to travel at warp speed !

Why couldn't the idiot's spaceship travel
at the speed of light ?

Because he took off in the dark !

What do you call dishonest spaceships ?

Lying saucers !

What sort of spaceships do secret agents fly in ?

Spying saucers !

What do you call miserable spaceships ?

Sighing saucers !

Which space villain looks like a pair of wellies ?

Darth Waders !

Where do you leave your spaceship whilst you visit another planet ?

At a parking meteor !

What sort of music do space aliens like best ?

Rocket and roll !

and

Heavy Metal !

Where do they lock up naughty space creatures ?

Jailien !

Why does Captain Kirk make the crew clean the Enterprise ?

He Likes things Spock and span !

Where do you sometimes hear singing in space ?

When you fly past a pop star !

Why did the alien build a spaceship from feathers ?

He wanted to travel light years !

Did you hear about the alien poet –
she wrote universes !

Why did Captain Kirk shave his head ?

To baldly go where no-one had been before !

Did you hear about the silly alien who
built a spaceship from herbs ?
He wanted to travel in Thyme !

What do alien footballers wear when
they arrive on Earth ?
Their landing strip !

What fast food do computers eat ?

Ram Burgers !

What piece of sports equipment does every alien own ?

A tennis rocket !

Why did the alien take a nuclear missile to the party?

In case he fancied blowing up some balloons!

Did you hear about the fat alien - he had to wear a 'not very much' space suit!

KNOCK KNOCK

Knock, knock...
Who's there ?
Bea...
Bea Who ?
Bea good boy and let me in !

Knock, knock...
Who's there ?
Yula...
Yula Who ?
Yula pologise for not letting me in straight
away when you see who it is !

Knock, knock...
Who's there ?
CD's...
CD's Who ?
CD's fingers ? They're freezing - let me in !

KNOCK KNOCK

Knock, knock...
Who's there ?
Wyatt...
Wyatt Who ?
**Wyatt you open the
door and see !**

Knock, knock...
Who's there ?
Ivan...
Ivan Who ?
**Ivan idea you will know
as soon as you
open the door !**

Knock, knock...
Who's there ?
Toyah...
Toyah Who ?
**Toyah have to ask
the same question
every time I come
round ?**

Knock, knock...
Who's there ?
Wynn...
Wynn Who ?
Wynn de Cleaner !

Knock, knock...
Who's there ?
Willy...
Willy Who ?
Willy lend me a street map, I'm a stranger in town !

Knock, knock...
Who's there ?
Bea...
Bea Who ?
Bea good boy and let me in !

Knock, knock...
Who's there ?
Stan...
Stan Who ?
Stan in front of the window and you'll see who !

Knock, knock...
Who's there ?
The Steps...
WOW - you mean the hit band ?
No, just the steps up to your front door !

Knock, knock...
Who's there ?
Paul...
Paul Who ?
Paul the door open a
bit, my coat is
trapped !

Knock, knock...
Who's there ?
Irma...
Irma Who ?
Irma little short of
time - just open up !

Knock, knock...
Who's there ?
Carrie...
Carrie Who ?
Carrie on like this and I'll have frozen
to death before I get in !

KNOCK KNOCK

Knock, knock...
Who's there ?
Fred...
Fred Who ?
Fred you'll have to open the door to find out !

Knock, knock...
Who's there ?
Vidor...
Vidor Who ?
Vidor better open soon....!

Knock, knock...
Who's there ?
Cole...
Cole Who ?
Cole out here - open up !

Knock, knock...
Who's there ?
Curley...
Curley Who ?
Curley self a good host -
keeping your guests
waiting out here !

Knock, knock...
Who's there ?
Ashley...
Bless you !

KNOCK KNOCK

Knock, knock...
Who's there ?
Freda...
Freda Who ?
Freda jolly good fellow...

Knock, knock...
Who's there ?
Holly...
Holly Who ?
Holly up and open the door, I'm fleezing out here !

Knock, knock...
Who's there ?
Piers...
Piers Who ?
Piers I've forgotten my
key - open up, there's a good chap !

Knock, knock...
Who's there ?
Julian...
Julian Who ?
Julian on that door all day waiting for
people to knock?

Knock, knock...
Who's there ?
Major...
Major Who ?
Major ask that question yet again didn't I !

Knock, knock...
Who's there ?
Sara...
Sara Who ?
Sara man delivering milk here yesterday - do you think he could deliver some to me too ?

Knock, knock...
Who's there ?
Joe...
Joe Who ?
Joe keep everybody waiting like this ?

Knock, knock...
Who's there ?
Tia...
Tia Who ?
Tia mount of time I've wasted standing here...!

Knock, knock...
Who's there ?
Norm...
Norm Who ?
Norm more Mr Nice Guy -
OPEN THIS DOOR !

Knock, knock...
Who's there ?
Giraffe...
Giraffe Who ?
Giraffe to ask such stupid questions ?

Knock, knock...
Who's there ?
Doctor...
Doctor Who ?
You've played this game before, haven't you ?

Knock, knock...
Who's there ?
Alpaca...
Alpaca Who ?
Alpaca suitcase and leave you if you
don't give me my own key !

KNOCK KNOCK

Knock, knock...
Who's there ?
Paula...
Paula Who ?
Paula door open for me, I've got
my hands full of shopping bags !

Knock, knock...
Who's there ?
Postman Pat...
Have you got a parcel ?
No, but I've got a black and white cat !

Knock, knock...
Who's there ?
London's...
London's who ?
Ah ! You cheated ! I'll bet you can hear
the animals from there !

Knock, knock...
Who's there ?
Lizard...
Lizard Who ?
Lizard - dobn't get too close, I'b
got a tebbible cold !

Knock, knock...
Who's there ?
Carib...
Carib Who ?
Was it the antlers that gave it away ?

KNOCK KNOCK

Knock, knock...
Who's there ?
Denise...
Denise Who ?
Denise are freezing in this short skirt !

Knock, knock...
Who's there ?
Isiah...
Isiah Who ?
Isiah than you - I'm up on the roof !

Knock, knock...
Who's there ?
Carla...
Carla Who ?
Carla doctor - I feel terrible !

Knock, knock...
Who's there ?
Mandy...
Mandy Who ?
Mandy with tools, if you need any repair work done !

Knock, knock...
Who's there ?
The Electricity Board also known as the George...
The Electricity Board also known as the George Who ?
**The Electricity Board also known as the
George of the light brigade !**

Knock, knock...
Who's there ?
Pop...
Pop Who ?
Pop down and unlock this door please !

Knock, knock...
Who's there ?
Jim...
Jim Who ?
Jim mind not asking the same old question
over and over !

Knock, knock...
Who's there ?
Carter...
Carter Who ?
Carter a long story short and open up !

Knock, knock...
Who's there ?
Alison...
Alison Who ?
Alison at the keyhole sometimes...

THE COLOSSAL KIDS' JOKE BOOK

Knock, knock...
Who's there ?
I Santa...
I Santa Who ?
I Santa message that I would
be here hours ago -
why is the door still locked ?

Knock, knock...
Who's there ?
Twit...
Twit who ?
Oh! Have you got a pet owl as well ?

Knock, knock...
Who's there ?
Ron...
Ron who ?
Ron away as fast as you can,
the aliens are coming...!

KNOCK KNOCK

Knock, knock...
Who's there ?
It's Lewis...
It's Lewis who ?
It's Lewis this door knob...I should get it fixed !

Knock, knock...
Who's there ?
Card...
Card who ?
Card seem to get my key to work in this look !

Knock, knock...
Who's there ?
Tai Ping...
Tai Ping who ?
Tai Ping these jokes is making my fingers ache !

Knock, knock...
Who's there ?
Noah...
Noah who ?
Noah anywhere I can shelter from this rain ?

Knock, knock...
Who's there ?
Yvonne...
Yvonne who ?
Yvonne to know you should open the door !

Knock, knock...
Who's there ?
Alpaca...
Alpaca who ?
Alpaca lunchbox for the train journey !

Knock, knock...
Who's there ?
Opera...
Opera who ?
Opera sock in it and open
the door for goodness sake !

Knock, knock...
Who's there ?
Carrie...
Carrie who ?
Carrie on like this and I'll be frozen to death
before you open the door !

Knock, knock...
Who's there ?
Alec...
Alec who ?
Alec the smell of fried egg and bacon
coming from your kitchen !

Knock, knock...
Who's there ?
Marge...
Marge who ?
Marge over to this door and open it, now !

Knock, knock...
Who's there ?
Lou...
Lou who ?
There's no need to cry - I just
want to come in !

Knock, knock...
Who's there ?
Carmen...
Carmen who ?
Carmen let me in please !

Knock, knock...
Who's there ?
Isiah...
Isiah who ?
Isiah than you, cos I'm standing on a box !

Knock, knock...
Who's there ?
Dinnah...
Dinnah who ?
Dinnah keep me waiting oot here its freezin !

Knock, knock...
Who's there ?
Les...
Les who ?
Les read this book again, it's brilliant !

Knock, Knock...
Who's there ?
Carmen
Carmen who ?
**Carmen to the front room and
look through the window !**

Knock, knock...
Who's there ?
Mort
Mort who ?
Mort have known you would ask me that !

Knock, Knock...
Who's there ?
It's Jilly
It's Jilly who ?
It's Jilly out here – let me in !

Knock, Knock...
Who's there ?
Acton
Acton who ?
Acton stupid won't do you any good !

Knock, Knock...
Who's there ?
Barker
Barker who ?
Barker door's locked so I've come round to the front !

Knock, Knock...
Who's there ?
Carrie
Carrie who ?
Carrie this shopping in for me, it weighs a ton !

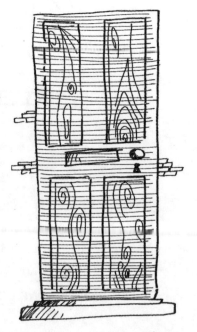

KNOCK KNOCK

Knock, Knock...
Who's there ?
Don
Don who ?
Don worry - I'm not a burglar !

Knock, Knock...
Who's there ?
Eddie
Eddie who ?
Eddie minute now I'm going to sneeze !

Knock, Knock...
Who's there ?
Fred
Fred who ?
Fred you'll have to open the door to find out !

Knock, Knock...
Who's there ?
Geoff
Geoff who ?
Geoff to ask that question every single day ?

Knock, Knock...
Who's there ?
Harry
Harry who ?
Harry up it's just starting
to rain !

Knock, Knock...
Who's there ?
Iona
Iona who ?
Iona a house just like this
one !

Knock, Knock...
Who's there ?
June
June who ?
June know how long I've
been waiting out here ?

Knock, Knock...
Who's there ?
Ken
Ken who ?
Ken you not guess ?

Knock, Knock...
Who's there ?
Can you Linda
Can you Linda who ?
Can you Linda me a cup of sugar ?

Knock, Knock...
Who's there ?
Mary
Mary who ?
Mary Christmas !

Knock, Knock...
Who's there ?
Nige
Nige who ?
Nige to see you, to see you Nige !

Knock, Knock...
Who's there ?
Oscar
Oscar who ?
**Oscar nother question for
goodness sake !**

KNOCK KNOCK

Knock, Knock...
Who's there ?
Pete
Pete who ?
Pete after me, 'I am going to open the door now...'

Knock, Knock...
Who's there ?
Ronnie
Ronnie who ?
Ronnie nose - need a hanky - let me in - quick !

Knock, Knock...
Who's there ?
Stella
Stella who ?
Stella same person who was here last time you asked !

Knock, Knock...
Who's there ?
Tone
Tone who ?
Tone keep asking me that same old question !

Knock, Knock...
Who's there ?
Unger
Unger who ?
Unger the doormat is where you'll find the key !

Knock, Knock...
Who's there ?
Val
Val who ?
Val how am I supposed to know ?!

KNOCK KNOCK

Knock, Knock...
Who's there ?
Wanda
Wanda who ?
**Wanda know - open the door
and find out !**

Knock, Knock...
Who's there ?
Xavier
Xavier who ?
**Xavier anything for
the jumble sale ?**

Knock, Knock...
Who's there ?
Annie
Annie who ?
**Annie chance you'll
open this door ?**

Knock, Knock...
Who's there ?
Barbara
Barbara who ?
Barbara black sheep !

Knock, Knock...
Who's there ?
Carla
Carla who ?
**Carla doctor, your door knocker has just fallen
off and broken my toe !**

Knock, Knock...
Who's there ?
Deb
Deb who ?
**Deb better be a good reason for keeping
me waiting out here!**
Knock, Knock...

KNOCK KNOCK

Who's there ?
Emma
Emma who ?
Emma not going to tell you again !

Knock, Knock...
Who's there ?
Fanny
Fanny who ?
Fanny how you always ask that question ?!

Knock, Knock...
Who's there ?
Arthur
Arthur who ?
Arthur gotten again !

Knock, Knock...
Who's there ?
Eileen Dover
Eileen Dover who ?
Eileen Dover your fence and broke it !

Knock, Knock...

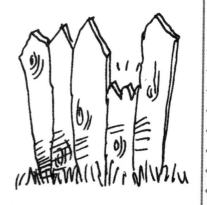

Who's there ?
Herbert
Herbert who ?
Herbert you come to the door and
see for yourself !

Knock, Knock...
Who's there ?
Morse
Morse who ?
Morse come in as quickly as possible !

Knock, Knock...
Who's there ?
Nipper
Nipper who ?
Nipper round the back and
pass my spectacles !

Knock, Knock...
Who's there ?
Oscar
Oscar who ?
Oscar a silly question...

Knock, Knock...
Who's there ?
Phil
Phil who ?
**Phil this cup with sugar would you,
I've just run out !**

EMPTY

Knock, Knock...
Who's there ?
Quad
Quad who ?
Quad you want to know for ?

Knock, Knock...
Who's there ?
Russell
Russell who ?
Russell be home in a
minute - put the kettle
on !

Knock, Knock...
Who's there ?
Sandy
Sandy who ?
Sandy you living next door innit ?!

Knock, Knock...
Who's there ?
Tamara
Tamara who ?
Tamara's my birthday, don't forget !

Knock, Knock...
Who's there ?
Urquart
Urquart who ?
Urquart just broke down, can you call the AA ?

Knock, Knock...
Who's there ?
Vera
Vera who ?
Vera long way from home and need a map !

Knock, Knock...
Who's there ?
Wendy
Wendy who ?
Wendy door finally opens you can see for yourself !

Knock, Knock...
Who's there ?
Xara
Xara who ?
Xara front door the same colour as this yesterday !

Knock, Knock...
Who's there ?
Posh
Posh who ?
Posh the door open and you'll see !
Knock, Knock...
Who's there ?
Euripides
Euripides who ?
**Euripides trousers you have to buy
some more !**

Knock, Knock...
Who's there ?
Ben
Ben who ?
**Ben down the supermarket, give us
a hand with these bags !**

Knock, Knock...
Who's there ?
Clara
Clara who ?
**Clara space for the shopping bags
like Ben told you to !**

Knock, Knock...
Who's there ?
Lucy
Lucy who ?
Lucy Lastic !

Knock, Knock...
Who's there ?
Miguel
Miguel who ?
Miguel friends packed me in !

Knock, Knock...
Who's there ?
Paul
Paul who ?
Paul the other one it's got bells on !

Knock, Knock...
Who's there ?
John
John who ?
John know I'm getting tired standing out here !

Knock, Knock...
Who's there ?
Wendy
Wendy who ?
Wendy door opens you'll see !

Knock, Knock...
Who's there ?
Moore
Moore who ?
Moore or less the same person as before !

Knock, Knock...
Who's there ?
Carrie
Carrie who ?
Carrie this suitcase upstairs for me...

KNOCK KNOCK

Knock, Knock...
Who's there ?
Julienne
Julienne who ?
Julienne against that front door all day ?

Knock, Knock...
Who's there ?
Carter
Carter who ?
Carter pillar !

Knock, Knock...
Who's there ?
Toulouse
Toulouse who ?
**Toulouse are better than
one in a busy house I
always say !**

Knock, Knock...
Who's there ?
**Double Glazing
Salesman.....hello.....hello...**

Knock, Knock...
Who's there ?
Furze
Furze who ?
Furze I'm concerned you can keep the door closed !

Knock, Knock...
Who's there ?
Germaine
Germaine who ?
Germaine I can't come in unless I tell you ?

Knock, Knock...
Who's there ?
Mush
Mush who ?
Mush you always ask me this ?

Knock, Knock...
Who's there ?
Hilda
Hilda who ?
Hilda 'owt for a laugh like, why aye !

KNOCK KNOCK

Knock, Knock...
Who's there ?
Mandy
Mandy who ?
Mandy lifeboats !

Knock, Knock...
Who's there ?
Frank
Frank who ?
Frank you for asking !

Knock, Knock...
Who's there ?
Egon
Egon who ?
Egon down the shops !

Knock, Knock...
Who's there ?
Harmony
Harmony who ?
**Harmony times do I have
to tell you ?!**

Knock, Knock...
Who's there ?
Sitter
Sitter who ?
Sitter good time to come round ?

Knock, Knock...
Who's there ?
Don
Don who ?
**Don be afraid....look
into my eyes.....you are
feeling sleepy...**

Knock, Knock...
Who's there ?
Ma
Ma who ?
Ma car broke down again !

Knock, Knock...
Who's there ?
A guest
A guest who ?
A guest you wouldn't recognise my voice !

KNOCK KNOCK

Knock, Knock...
Who's there ?
Arnie
Arnie who ?
Arnie chance of coming in ?

Knock, Knock...
Who's there ?
Dan
Dan who ?
Dan Dan Dan Dan Daaaannnn !

Knock, Knock...
Who's there ?
Carrie
Carrie who ?
**Carrie on like this and
I'll freeze to death out
here !**

Knock, Knock...
Who's there ?
Hal
Hal who ?
Halloo !

Knock, Knock...
Who's there ?
A ghost
A ghost who ?
Thought it would scare you !

Knock, Knock...
Who's there ?
Kenya
Kenya who ?
Kenya please just open the door !?

Knock, Knock...
Who's there ?
France
France who ?
France y meeting you here !

Who's there ?
Moses
Moses who ?
**Moses you have to let me in without
asking stupid questions !**

Knock, Knock...
Who's there ?
Adolf
Adolf who ?
Adolf ball hit me in de mouf !

Knock, Knock...
Who's there ?
Chris
Chris who ?
Chris Packet, but my friends call me Russell !

Knock, Knock...
Who's there ?
Iona
Iona who ?
Iona have eyes for you !

Knock, Knock...
Who's there ?
Tinkerbell
Tinkerbell who ?
Tinkerbell would look nice on my bike !

Knock, Knock...
Who's there ?
Justin
Justin who ?
Just in time to open the door for me !

Knock, Knock...
Who's there ?
Maquis
Maquis who ?
Maquis just snapped in the lock !

Knock, Knock...
Who's there ?
Isabell
Isabell who ?
Isabell not working ?

Knock, Knock...
Who's there ?
Jethro
Jethro who ?
Jethro people out if they can't pay their bill ?

Knock, Knock...
Who's there ?
Amos
Amos who ?
Amosquito bit me !

Knock, Knock...
Who's there ?
Lettuce
Lettuce who ?
Lettuce in and you'll find out !

Knock, Knock...
Who's there ?
Ivor
Ivor who ?
**Ivor message for a
Mr Smith ?!**

Knock, Knock...
Who's there ?
Sid
Sid who ?
Sid down next to me !

Knock, Knock...
Who's there ?
Shirley
Shirley who ?
Shirley you know the sound of my voice by now ?

Knock, Knock...
Who's there ?
Midas
Midas who ?
Midas well open the door and find out !

Knock, Knock...
Who's there ?
Jester
Jester who ?
Jester minute I've forgotten !

Knock, Knock...
Who's there ?
Sinbad
Sinbad who ?
Sinbad condition your front door !

Knock, Knock...
Who's there ?
Harry
Harry who ?
Harry up and let me in !

KNOCK KNOCK

Knock, Knock...
Who's there ?
Caine
Caine who ?
Caine you see me through the glass ?

Knock, Knock...
Who's there ?
Yul
Yul who ?
Yul find out when you open the door

Knock, Knock...
Who's there ?
Cattle
Cattle who ?
Cattle get out if you open the door.
I'll come in through the window !

Knock, Knock...
Who's there ?
And your old lady
And your old lady who ?
I didn't know you could yodel !

Knock, Knock...
Who's there ?
Doris
Doris who ?
Doris closed - that's why I'm having to knock !

Knock, Knock...
Who's there ?
Europe
Europe who ?
Europe bright and early today !

KNOCK KNOCK

Knock, Knock...
Who's there ?
Orang
Orang who ?
Orang the doorbell but it doesn't seem to
work, so now I'm knocking !

Knock, Knock...
Who's there ?
Alf
Alf who ?
Alf feed the cat while you're on holiday !

Knock, Knock...
Who's there ?
Stephanie
Stephanie who ?
Stephanie me - who else could it be !

Knock, Knock...
Who's there ?
Witch doctor
Witch doctor who ?
The one with the long stripy scarf !

Knock, Knock...
Who's there ?
Wooden shoe
Wooden shoe who ?
Wooden shoe like to see ?

Knock, Knock...
Who's there ?
May-Belle
May-Belle who ?
May-Belle don't work either, so I'm knocking !

KNOCK KNOCK

Knock, Knock...
Who's there ?
Noah
Noah who ?
Noah a good place to hide from this rain ?

Knock, Knock...
Who's there ?
Will
Will who ?
Will I ever get in !?

Knock, Knock...
Who's there ?
Luke
Luke who ?
Luke out - the Martians are landing !

Knock, Knock...
Who's there ?
Mindy
Mindy who ?
Mindy porch !

Knock, Knock...
Who's there ?
Othello
Othello who ?
Othello could freeze to death out here !

Knock, Knock...
Who's there ?
Fools Rachid
Fools Rachid who ?
Fools Rachid where angels fear to tread !

KNOCK KNOCK

Knock, Knock...
Who's there ?
Oasis
Oasis who ?
Oasis, it's your brother,
I forget me key !

Knock, Knock...
Who's there ?
Mickey
Mickey who ?
Mickey don't fit - have you
changed the lock ?

Knock, Knock...
Who's there ?
Kong
Kong who ?
Kong ratulations you've won the lottery !

Knock, Knock...
Who's there ?
Moss
Moss who ?
Moss be time to move onto the next section !!

SPOOKY

Why do window cleaners hate vampires?

They are a pane in the neck!

hich window cleaners do vampires use ?

The one in pane - sylvania !

Why do monsters like to stand in a ring ?

They love being part of a vicious circle !

What do you call a ghostly teddy bear ?

Winnie the OOOooooooOooooohhHHhhhhh !

Why did the vampire go to the blood donor centre ?

To get lunch !

What do you call a Welsh ghost ?

Dai !

What do you call a tough Welsh ghost that stars in an action movie ?

Dai Hard !

Why did the England cricket team consult a vampire ?

They wanted to put some bite into the opening bats !

How do vampires start a duel ?

They stand Drac to Drac !

When do ghosts wear red jackets and ride horses ?

When they go out fox haunting !

Why are owls so brave at night ?

Because they don't give a hoot for
ghosts, monsters or vampires !

What did the old vampire say when he broke his teeth ?

Fangs for the memory !

Why do vampires holiday at the seaside ?

They love to be near the ghostguard stations !

What is the ghostly Prime Minister called ?

Tony Scare !

What do you call a dentist who really likes vampires ?

An extractor fan !

What do you call a
futuristic android
who comes back in
time to plant seeds?

Germinator!

And what do you
call his twin brother?

Germinator II!

What do you call the ghost of the handkerchief?

The Bogie man!

What sort of wolf can you wear?

A wear wolf!

What sort of wolf delivers Christmas presents?

Santa Claws!

What do you call a lazy skeleton ?

Bone Idle !

What do you call a ghostly would-be Scottish King ?

Boney Prince Charlie !

Why do ghosts catch cold so easily ?

They get chilled to the marrow !

What do you call a scary, boney creature that
staggers around making strange wailing noises?

A supermodel making a record!

Why are skeletons no good at telling lies?

Because you can see right through them!

What should you say when a vampire
gives you a present?

Fang you very much!

Why don't vampires like modern things ?

Because they hate anything new fangled !

Why did the ghost get the job he applied for ?

He was clearly the best candidate !

What do you call a ghostly haircut with long curly strands of hair ?

Deadlocks !

What do ghosts like with their food ?

A little whine !

What film is about a scary train robber ?

Ghost Buster !

Where do ghosts live ?

In flats !

Where do vampires like to go for their holidays ?

The Dead Sea !

Why did the two vampire bats get married ?

Because they were heels over heads in love !

What did the pirate get when he smashed
a skeleton up in a fight ?

A skull and very cross bones !

Where do skeletons cook their meals ?

In a skullery !

What do you call a young
skeleton in a cap and uniform ?

A skullboy !

Why did the skeleton fall into a hole?

It was a grave mistake!

What villain does the spooky 007 fight?

Ghoulfinger!

Why are hyenas always falling out?

They always have a bone to pick with each other!

Who delivers Christmas presents to vampires?

Sack-ula!

What vampire can you wear to protect
you from the rain ?

Mac - ula !

What is the fairy tale about a girl who
falls in love with a really ugly loaf of bread ?

Beauty and the yeast !

When they got married, what sort of children
did they have ?

Bun-shees !

Why did Goldilocks go to Egypt ?

She wanted to see the *mummy* bear !

AND, SPEAKING OF MUMMIES...

Mummy, mummy, what is a vampire?

Be quiet and eat your soup before it clots!

Mummy, mummy, what is a werewolf?

Be quiet and comb your face!

Mummy, mummy
I don't like my
uncle Fred!

Well, just leave
him on the side
of your plate
and eat
the chips!

Mummy, mummy I don't want to go to America!

Be quiet and keep swimming!

Mummy, mummy I'm just going out for a quick
bite to eat !

OK, but make sure you're back in your
coffin before daybreak !

What did the monster say when the vampire asked for his
daughter's hand in marriage ?

OK, we'll eat the rest !

Why do some ghosts paint themselves
with black and white stripes ?

So they can frighten people on Pelican crossings !

OR

So they can play for Boocastle United !

What should you wear when you go out
for a drink with a vampire ?

A metal collar !

What do you call a young woman who hunts vampires ?

A Miss Stake !

What do the police call it when they
watch a vampire's house ?

A stake out !

What does the monster Tarzan eat for tea ?

Snake and pygmy pie with chips !

What did the ghostly show jumper always score ?

A clear round !

What did the young ghost call his mum and dad ?

His trans-parents !

Why don't you have to worry what you say to the werewolf computer engineer ?

His bark is worse than his byte !

What sort of jokes do werewolves like best ?

Howlers !

What happens when a werewolf meets a vampire ?

He doesn't turn a hair !

Why wasn't the werewolf allowed to get
off the lunar spaceship ?

Because the moon was full !

Why did the werewolf start going to the gym ?

Because he liked the changing rooms !

What did the train driver say to the werewolf?

Keep the change!

Why did the werewolf steal underwear
when the moon was full?

Because his doctor told him a change
was as good as a vest!

What sort of news do werewolves fear?

Silver bulletins!

Why did the shy werewolf hide in a cupboard
every full moon ?

Because he didn't like anyone to see him changing !

What form of self defence do werewolves use ?

Coyote !

How do mummies knock on doors ?

They wrap as hard as they can !

Why was the mummy done up in brightly coloured sparkly
paper ?

He was gift-wrapped !

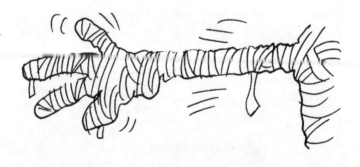

What does it say on the *mummy's* garage entrance ?

Toot, and come in !

What do *mummies* use to fasten things together ?

A Hammer and Niles !

What do children in Egypt call their parents ?

Mummy and Daddy of course !

Why was the Egyptian Prince worried?

Because his *mummy* and daddy were both mummies!

What do mummies shout when they are on a sinking boat?

A bandage ship!

What do mummies do to relax?

They just unwind a little!

Why was the *mummy's* leg stiff?

Because someone had been winding him up!

SPOOKY

What are the scariest dinosaurs?

Terror dactyls!

Why are mummies good
at keeping secrets?

**They can keep things
under wraps for
centuries!**

Why did the werewolf
go out at the
full moon?

**Because his doctor
told him that a
change would
do him good!**

What did the ghost
of the owl say?

**Too-wit too-
wooooooooooooo....**

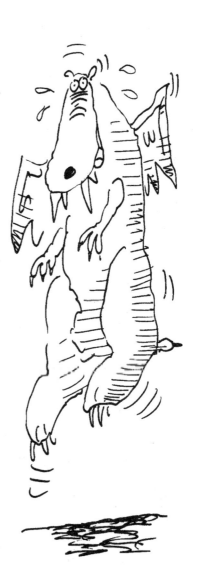

Why is Godzilla sitting on a friend like leaving home ?

Because you end up with a flat mate !

Who was the winner of the headless horse race ?

No-one, they all finished neck and neck !

What did the President of the USA say to the giant ape when he won the lottery?

Kong - ratulations !

What eats your letters when you post them ?

A ghost box !

What spook delivers your letters ?

Ghostman Pat and his skeleton cat !

Which creature saves people from drowning ?

The Ghostguard !

Why did the vampire like eating chewy sweets ?

He liked something to get his teeth into !

Why do sausages and bacon spit when
they are being cooked ?

Because it's a terror frying experience !

What is the scariest thing you could find in your
Christmas stocking ?

The ghost of Christmas presents !

Why did the vampire put tomato ketchup
on his sandwiches ?

He was a vegetarian !

How do you grow a werewolf from a seed ?

Just use plenty of fur-tiliser !

Why can you never get through to a vampire
bat on the telephone ?

Because they always hang up !

What football teams does Dracula support ?

Shiverpool !

Fang-chester United !

Scream Park Rangers !

What football team does Frankenstein's
monster support ?

Bolt - On Wanderers !

THE COLOSSAL KIDS' JOKE BOOK

What is a werewolf's favourite film ?

The Full Moonty !

What lies at the bottom of the sea and shivers ?

A nervous wreck !

Which vampire likes playing practical jokes ?

Dracu-lark !

Where do vampires keep their savings ?

In a blood bank or the ghost office !

What did Jeremy Paxman say to the werewolf team on University Challenge?

No con-furring!

What pop group did the young mummies join?

A boy bandage!

What would you call a mummified cat?

A first aid kit!

Why was Dracula ill after biting someone on a train home from work?

He caught a commuter virus!

If hairy palms is the first sign of turning into
a monster, what is the second ?

Looking for them !

How do you stop a werewolf attacking you ?

Throw a stick for it to fetch !

What was on the haunted aeroplane ?

An air ghostess and a lot of high spirits !

Why couldn't the ghost get a whisky
in the pub after 11 o'clock ?

Because they aren't allowed to serve
spirits after closing time !

Why did the witch take her small
book of magic on holiday ?

The doctor told her to get away for a little spell !

Who was the fattest mummy ever ?

Two ton Carmen !

Why couldn't the witches victim move ?

He was spellbound !

How can you spot a sea monster ?

He's the one with the wavy hair !

What do sea monsters eat ?

Fish and ships !

Why do sea monsters go to so many parties ?

They like to have a whale of a time !

Which sea monster rules the waves ?

The Cod-father !

What do baby sea monsters play with ?

Doll-fins !

What do you give a monster that feels sick?

Plenty of room!

Where do monsters sleep?

Anywhere they want to!

What do you get if a monster falls over in a car park?

Traffic jam!

What would you get if you combined a monster,
a vampire, a werewolf and a ghost?

As far away as possible!

What do monsters call a crowded swimming pool ?

Soup !

What do you get if you shoot a werewolf with a silver bullet ?

A very interesting rug !

What do you call the ghost of a werewolf that lives at the seaside ?

A Clear - Pier - Were - Wolf !

How did Frankenstein's monster escape from the police ?

He made a bolt for it !

Why did Dracula visit a psychiatrist ?

He thought he was going batty !

What sort of music do vampires and ghosts like best ?

Haunted House Music !

If a monster buys you a chair for your birthday
should you accept it ?

Yes - but don't let him plug it in !

What does a monster shout when it is scared ?

Mummy !

Can you stick vampires to your window ?

Yes - they are suckers !

Why did the ghost go to the bicycle shop ?

He needed some new spooks for his front wheel !

Where do ghouls live ?

Bury !

What game do ghouls play ?

Bury St Edmonds !

What do you call a stupid vampire ?

A clot !

What sort of jobs do spooks like?

Dead end jobs!

What do ghosts do at parties?

They have a wail of a time!

Who do vampires invite to their birthday parties?

Anybody they can dig up!

Why don't ghosts go out during the day ?

They are scared of people !

Why don't skeletons have glass eyes ?

Because they come out in conversation !

Why are vampires always cheerful ?

Because they are terrified of being cross !

What is a werewolves favourite film ?

Claws !

What sort of voice do werewolves have?

Husky ones!

What do werewolves hate most?

When people lead them a dog's life!

What do you get if you cross a vampire with
a knight of the round table ?

A Bite in shining armour !

What was Dr Frankenstein best at ?

Making new friends !

What do spooks eat in the morning ?

A hearty breakfast of Dreaded Wheat !

Why didn't the vampire laugh at the joke
about the wooden stake ?

He didn't get the point !

What do you get if you cross the Abominable
Snowman and Count Dracula ?

Severe frostbite !

Where do spooks go shopping ?

In BOOOO-tiques !

What did the spook begin his letter with?

Tomb it may concern....

Where is the invisible man?

No idea, I haven't seen him around for ages!

What did the sign in the pyramid shop say?

Satisfaction guaranteed or your mummy back!

Why are vampires so thin?

They eat necks to nothing!

Why did the ghoul take so long
to finish his newspaper?

He wasn't very hungry!

Why did the monster eat a settee and two
armchairs?

He had developed a suite tooth!

Why did the vampire bats hangingin the
church belfry look exactly the same
as each other ?

They were dead ringers !

Why didn't the spook win the lottery ?

He didn't have a ghost of a chance !

Why did the ghost of Guy Fawkes go crazy ?

It's OK, he just lost his head for a moment !

Wow - did you see that wolf ?

Where ?

No - it was just an ordinary one !

What sport do monsters like best ?

Sculling !

How do you know when there is a horrible monster under your bed ?

You don't - that's what makes it so very scary !

What do you call an overweight vampire?

Draculard!

What do monsters eat for breakfast?

Human beans on toast!

How many skeletons can you fit in an empty coffin ?

Just one - after that it's not empty any more !

What did the *mummy* ghost say to the little ghost ?

Don't spook until you're spooken to !

Where would you find a suitable gift for
a tortured ghost ?

In a chain store !

What kind of ice cream do vampires like best ?

Necktarine flavour !

Why did the vampire but a computer ?

He wanted to get onto the interneck !

What day of the week do vampires and werewolves like best ?

Moonday - especially full-moonday !

What sort of ghost would you find up your nose ?

A Bogeyman !

How do you know if there is a ghost in a hotel ?

Ask to see the hotel in - spectre !

Why should you never run if you see a werewolf ?

Because they go mad for fast food !

What sort of music do ghosts like best ?

Haunting melodies !

How do mummies go into their pyramids ?

Gift wrapped !

Why did the zombie go to the chemists ?

He wanted something to stop his coffin !

How do you get a mummy interested in music ?

Play him some wrap !

What should you never order if you're
eating out with a vampire ?

Steak and chips !

EEK!

What is a ghosts' favourite creature ?

The Whale !

Why do ghosts go back to the same place
every year for their holidays ?

They like their old haunts best !

VAMPIRE HUNTERS MENU. . .

GARLIC BREAD

followed by

HAMMERED STEAK

and finally

HOT CROSS BUNS

What do you call a ghost that doesn't scare anyone ?

A failure !

What does a well brought up vampire say
after he has bitten your neck ?

Fang you very much !

VAMPIRE SAYINGS...

Once bitten - twice bitten !

A neck in your hand is worth two in a bush !

A stitch in time - means I can come back for some more !

There's many a slip 'twixt neck and lip !

What is a skeleton ?

A body with the person scraped off !

What does a skeleton feed his dog?

Anything but bones !!

Why do skeletons take a dog with them to the seaside?

They need something to bury them in the sand !

Why do skeletons drink lots of milk?

Because calcium is good for your bones !

What do skeletons eat on Good Friday ?

Hot Cross Bones !

Why do skeletons dislike horror films ?

Because they scare them to the marrow !

What sort of jokes do skeletons enjoy ?

Rib ticklers !

What do skeletons sing at birthday parties ?

Femur jolly good fellow. . .

Why was the skeleton's jacket in shreds ?

Because he had very sharp shoulder blades !

What do skeleton schoolchildren wear ?

Knee caps !

What do vampires eat at parties ?

Fang Furters !

What do you call a very old vampire ?

A Gran-pire !

How do vampires and ghosts go on holiday ?

By Scareyplane !

What did the teacher say to the naughty vampires in class ?

Stop Draoularking about !

Did you hear about the ghost who cut down trees at three o'clock in the morning?

He was the thing that made stumps in the night!

What do you call twin ghosts?

Dead ringers!

Why was the vampire lying dead on the floor of the restaurant?

It was a steak house!

What does a young boy ghost do to get a girlfriend?

He wooooooooos her!

What are the only jobs that skeletons can get?

Skeleton staff!

What about the two ghosts who got married –
it was love at first fright!

What do ghosts do if they are afraid?
Hide under a sheet!

What is the difference between a ghost
and a custard cream biscuit?

Have you tried dipping a ghost in your tea?!

How does a skeleton know when it's going to rain ?

He just gets a feeling in his bones !

What is . . . visible - invisible - visible - invisible - visible - invisible ?

A skeleton on a zebra crossing !

Where do vampires get washed ?

In the bat room !

What room must all werewolf homes have ?

A changing room !

What sort of shampoo do ghosts use ?

Wash and Groan !

Why did the skull go to the disco on his own ?

He had no body to go with !

GHASTLY GHOSTLY SAYINGS...

Two's company - threes a shroud !

Never kick a ghost while he's down -
your foot will just go through him !

He who laughs last - obviously hasn't
seen the ghost standing behind him !

What do ghosts watch on TV ?

Scare Trek !

Horror Nation Street !

Bone and Away !

The Booos at Ten !

Sesame Sheet !

Have I got whoooos for you !

and, of course. . .

Till Death Us Do Part !

What can you use to flatten a ghost ?

A spirit level !

Why did the ghosts have a party ?

They wanted to lift their spirits !

What do ghosts carry their luggage in
when they go on holiday?

Body bags!

What do skeletons learn about at school?

Decimals and Fractures!

SKELEMENU...

Ox-Tail Soup

followed by

Spare Ribs and Finger Buffet

finishing with

Marrowbone Jelly and Custard!

Where does a vampire keep his money?

In a blood bank!

What do you call an overweight vampire ?

Draculard !

What do you call a vampire who has been in the pub ?

Drunkula !

What do you call a vampire that hides in the kitchen ?

Spatula !

What do you call a vampire mummy ?

Wrapula !

What do you call a young vampire ?

Draculad !

What do you call a vampire that attacks insects ?

A cricket bat !

What do you call a monster airline steward ?

A Fright attendant !

What do monsters eat ?

Shepherds Pie
and
Ploughmans Lunch

Why are monsters always falling out
with each other ?

There's always a bone of contention !

What was the name of the monster in the 3 bears ?

Ghouldilocks !

What are a monsters favourite fairground rides ?

The Helter Skeleton !

or the

Roller Ghoster !

Which monster is the most untidy ?

The Loch Mess Monster

What songs do they play at ghostly discos ?

Haunting melodies !

What does a young monster call his parents ?

Mummy and Deady !

Mum, I've decided I don't like my brother after all !

Well, just eat the chips and leave him on the side of the plate !

Why was the monster catching centipedes ?

He wanted scrambled legs for breakfast !

What game do ghostly mice play at parties ?

Hide and Squeak !

Where do monsters live ?

Crawley !

Why did the monster buy an axe ?

Because he wanted to get ahead in life !

Why did the monster eat his music teacher ?

His Bach was worse than his bite !

Why was the monster scared of the computer?

Because its memory had a killer bite!

What position do monsters play in football?

They are the ghoul posts!

Why do monsters have lots of nightmares?

They like to take their work
to bed with them!

What game do young monsters play ?

Corpse and Robbers !

What do monsters like to pour on their Sunday dinner ?

Grave - y !

Where do monster go on their American holidays ?

Death Valley !

How does Frankenstein's monster eat ?

He bolts his food down !

Why should you never touch a monster's tail ?

Because it is the end of the monster,
and it could also be the end of you !

Why did the monster comedian like playing to skeletons ?

Because he knew how to tickle their funny bones !

During which age did
mummies live ?

The Band - Age !

Eat your sprouts, son,
they'll put colour in
your cheeks !

But I don't want green
cheeks !

What do you call a monster that comes to your home to collect your laundry ?

An Undie-taker !

What is the first thing a monster does when you give him an axe ?

Writes out a chopping list !

Which room in your home can ghouls not enter ?

The living room !

Why did the monster have twins in his lunchbox ?

In case he fancied seconds !

What job could a young monster do ?

Chop assistant !

How did the monster cook the local hairdresser ?

On a barbercue !

What do monsters like for breakfast ?

Dreaded Wheat !

What did the metal monster have on his gravestone ?

Rust In Peace !

What do monsters have at tea time ?

Scream cakes !

What did the mummy monster say to her child a
t the dining table ?

Don't spook with your mouth full !

What is a young monsters favourite TV programme ?

BOO Peter !

Why didn't the skeleton fight the monster ?

He didn't have the guts !

Why was the monster hanging round
the pond with a net ?

He was collecting the ingredients for toad in the hole !

Where do skeletons keep their money ?

In a joint account !

What film did the monster James Bond star in ?

Ghouldfinger !

What has 50 legs ?

A centipede cut in half !

What sort of curry do monsters make
from their victims hearts ?

Tikka !

SOME MONSTER HOLIDAYS...

Good Fryday !
(Good for frying anyone who gets close enought to
grab !)

Eater Sunday and Eater Monday !
(Monsters don't have eggs !)

Guy Forks Night !

(Stay at home on November 5th if you are called Guy !)

Crisps and Eve !
(Another traditional monster recipe !)

Why are monsters
so horrible ?

It's in the blood !

Why do monsters breed fish with hands ?

So they can have fish fingers with their chips !

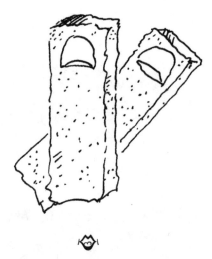

What do monsters eat if the catch someone
breaking into their home ?

Beef burglars !

What do monsters make with cars ?

Traffic jam !

Why do monsters never eat police officers ?

They hate truncheon meat !

Did you hear about the monster who asked if he could leave the dining table ?

His mum said yes, should would put it in the fridge and he could eat it later !

WWhat do Italian monsters eat ?

Spookgetti !

Some foreign holiday resorts favoured by monsters...

Eat a Lee !

Belch um !

Gnaw Wayne !

Sweet Den

What do ehadless monsters eat ?

Chops !

Which monster monkey thinks he can sing ?

King Song !

Whay do you call a monster with an
axe buried in his head ?

Nothing - it's perfectly normal for monsters !

Who patrols the graveyard at night ?

A fright watchman !

Why did the monster have twins in his lunchbox ?

In case he wanted seconds !

What did the policeman say to the
monster with three heads ?

Hello, hello, hello !

ALPHABET

Fan Belt

Something that keeps a football
supporter's trousers up!

A

Aardvark	A vark that thinks it's tough !
Abdomen	Men with beer bellies !

Abigail	Strong wind heard in a monastery !
Absent minded	Oh ! I seem to have forgotten this one !?
Absolute	The best musical instrument in the World, ever !
Abundance	Disco for cakes !
Accidental	When you fall and knock your teeth out on the way to the dentists !

Address	Something a woman wears at her wedding !
Angler	Someone who is good at maths !
Antifreeze	An Inuit's mum's sister !
Aromatic	Early machine for making arrows !
Astronaut	When a spaceman scores nothing in his maths exam !
Attendance	Dance for 10 people !
Audio Visual	Sign language !
Automate	When your best friend is a robot !

BEST BUD

B

Backgammon	Game played by pigs !
Bacteria	The rear entrance to a cafeteria !
Baked Alaska	The result of global warming !
Balderdash	Running away from a crazy hairdresser !
Bandsaws	Blisters on guitarist's fingers !
Bandage	The average age of a pop group !
Banshee	Don't let that ghost in here !
Barber	Sheep trained as a hairdresser !

Barbecue   An outdoor party for sheep !

Bashful   Someone who has been in a fight !

Bathtub   Part of a fat man that never goes underwater in the bath !

Beckon   Send footballer on to the pitch !

Beehive   What mummy bees tell naughty bees to do !

Beeline   What naughty bees get at school !

Belladonna   Telephone a girl called Donna !

Bernadette   Set fire to your bills !

Betwixt   Halfway through a chocolate bar !

Big Top	Large hat worn by circus ringmaster !
Bindweed	Tie up a weak person !
Bird of Prey	Eagle that goes to church every Sunday !
Birkenhead	Not very intelligent !
Blockade	Stop lemonade being delivered !
Blood Brother	Vampire's relative !
Brain Wave	Permed hair !

C

Cabinet Pudding	School pudding made from furniture !
Cagoule	Ghost who goes around in a car !

Calculate	Finish maths test ages after everyone else !
Campus	Cat that lives in a college !
Capstan	Put Stan's hat on !
Carnivore	Animal that eats cars !
Carousel	Car that goes round in circles !
Cartoon	Song sung by cars !
Cat Burglar	Burglar who steals cats !
Caterpillar	Where a cat sleeps !
Cauliflower	Dog with a bunch of roses !
Celery	Wages paid to a gardener !

Cheapskate	Skateboard for a budgie !
Chilli Powder	Fine snowflakes !
Christmas Island	Where Santa spends the Summer !
Chrysanthemum	Christopher and one parent !
Circumference	The knight who designed the round table !
Cliff Hanger	Where a giant leaves his coat !
Coarse fish	Bad mannered fish !
Coat of Arms	Monster's coat with 13 sleeves !
Commentator	Any potato that isn't a Jersey Royal or King Edward !
Crime Wave	Where robbers go to surf !
Czeck -	Money paid into a foreign bank account !

ALPHABET

D

Dab Hand	Someone who is very good at finger painting !
Daft	Covered in daffodils !
Dandruff	Mrs Druff's husband !
Dark Ages	A time when there were lots of knights !
Deadline	Fence around a graveyard !
Deception	The door that leads out of reception !
Deck Chair	Chair made from beach !
Defence	Something that runs round the garden !
Depend	The end of the swimming pool with most water !
Dessert Spoon	Spoon for eating sand !
Diagnosis	What you get from a Welsh doctor !
Disband	Break up a pop group !
Disconcerted	Thrown out of a concert !

Dispense   Give out pocket money !

Dissent   Say you don't like someone's perfume !

Dogmatic   Robot dog !

Dungarees   Trousers worn for shifting manure !

E

Earwigs   Hair that old people grow out of their ears !

Eclipse   What the Martian gardener does with his hedges !

Editor   Teacher who can throw chalk accurately over 25 metres !

Effortless   Sleeping through an exam !

Elastic band   Group who play rubber instruments !

Elderberry	Oldest berry on the plant !
Electric Eel	Fish that swims in strong currents !
Emphasis	When your sister shouts at you !
Emulate	Ostrich pretending to be an Emu !
Engraving	Vampire's hobby !
Evaporated	Dried water - just add liquid !
Experiment	What scientists did 100 years ago and you are still doing in school !
Explosion	Result of experiment !
Eyecatching	Game played by monsters !

F

Factory	Place where they make trees !
Fail Safe	Safe with a broken lock !
Family Tree	Place where ghouls bury each other for a laugh !
Fan Belt	What a football supporter uses to keep his trousers up !
Father In Law	Dad in jail !
Feed Back	When a vampire bites you from behind !
Fertile	Tiles in a werewolf's house !
Fetlock	Padlock for a horse !
Filbert	Give Albert his dinner !
Fireworks	Sack everybody in the factory !
Fish Fingers	What fish have 5 of on each hand !
Flagstone	Stone age Union Jack !
Flash bulb	A light bulb that thinks very highly of itself !

Flashback	What happens when you hold the camera back to front !
Flea Market	Where fleas do their shopping !
Flight Deck	The pack of cards used by pilots !
Fly by Night	Vampire Owl !
Flying Colours	Paint thrown in art lesson !
Flypaper	What flies decorate their homes with !
Forward Roll	The 3 day old sandwich pushed to the front to make you buy it !
Foul Mouthed	Bad language from a chicken !

Four Poster	Bedroom with 4 posters on the wall !
Frog March	What frog soldiers do !

G

Galleon	Fuel measure for old ships !
Gamekeeper	Teacher who confiscates computer games in class !
Gargoyle	Pulling faces when gargling !
Generation Gap	The distance you keep behind your parents when they do something embarrassing, like dancing in supermarkets !
Gherkin	Relatives of a Gher !
Gladiator	How a monster felt after lunch !
Goal Mouth	Someone shouting from behind the nets !
Green Belt	Something which holds your pants up with recycled materials !
Gripe Water	The sort of rain that makes people complain !

H

Hacking Jacket	Coat worn for cutting hedges and trees !
Haggis	Eaten by witches in Scotland !
Hair Restorer	Vet !
Harvest	What farmers wear to cut corn !
Hatch Back	Car boot full of eggs !
Heart Warming	Monster's cooking class !
Heirloom	Weaving machine for rabbits !
Hog Wash	Pig in a bath !

Home Sick   Fed up being at home in the summer holidays !

Honeycomb   What bees use to style their hair !

Hoodwink   What Robin Hood did to Maid Marian !

Hoot Owl   Bird that doesn't care about anything !

Hopscotch   Sword dance in bare feet !

Humbug   Insect that can't remember the words !

Hysterical   Funny version of History !

I

Ice Cap   What your knee is when you fall on it when ice skating !

Ice lolly   What they use for money at the North Pole !

Icicle   A bicycle with a bit missing !

Ideogram   Telegram sent to an idiot !

Identical   Twins who laugh at the same time when you tickle them !

Illiteracy   Disease caught from books !

Ignite	Eskimo's bedtime !
Impatient	Someone fidgeting in the doctor's waiting room !
Impeccable	Hidden away from birds !
Impediment	Broken bicycle !
Impersonate	Cannibals dinner guest !
Introduce	Orange drink served at start of match !

Italic	Italian smart alec !

J

Jackdaw	Lift a car up by the door handle !
Jam Packed	A car full of strawberry jam !

Jargon	A missing jar of strawberry jam !
Jelly Beans	What jelly babies have on toast !
Jitterbug	Tense insect !
Joan of Arc	Noah's mum !
Jodhpurs	Trousers worn by a cat !
Joint Account	The bank where Frankenstein keeps all his spare parts !
Juggernaut	Empty jug !

K

Karate   Self defence for mice !

Kenya   Can you ?

Kerb Drill   Machine used for making holes in pavement !

Kerchief   King of all the hankies !

Kettle Drum What musicians make tea in !

Kidnap   Sleeping baby !

Kilocycle   Really hard bike to ride !

Kipper   Fish that is always asleep !

Korma   What you end up in if someone drops a pan
                 of curry on your head !

L

Labrador	Large cat-flap for dogs !
Lady-In-Waiting	Woman in queue outside loo !
Lambda	Greek letter invented by a sheep !

Lapdog	Greyhound used in racing !
Last Minute	Longest 60 seconds of the whole school day !
Laughing Stock	Funny Oxo cube !
Launch Pad	Throw notebook at someone !
Lazy Bones	Idle skeleton !

Lemon Squash   When an elephant sits down in a greengrocers !

Leopard Lily   A flower no-one wants to smell !

Lie Detector   Head teacher !

Linesman   Bad tempered teacher !

M

Macintosh   Waterproof Computer !

Magician   Anyone who can score more than 14% in a maths examination !

Magic Eye   What teachers have in the back of their heads !

Magneto   Italian for magnet !

ALPHABET

Mental Cruelty	Double maths on Friday afternoon !
Metronome	Musical elf driving a Mini !
Metacarpus	Scene of an accident involving a motor vehicle and a cat !
Minimum	Metronome's mother !
Microwave	Very small cooker !
Milk Chocolate	Something that no-one can do !
Milk Shake	What you get from nervous cows !
Misprint	Copy someone else's homework incorrectly !
Mistletoe	What Santa gets when he drops his sleigh on his foot !
Mitten	What a cat has when it swallows a ball of wool !
Moment of Truth	Exam results !
Mortar Board	What teachers who used to be bricklayers wear !
Mothball	What moths play football with !
Multi Storey	Very tall library !

Mummy   Egyptian child's daddy !

Mumbo Jumbo   Elephant who doesn't speak clearly !

MUMBLE...
MUTTER...

Mushroom   The room where all the Eskimos go to train their husky dogs to pull sleds. You will often hear the word 'mush' as you walk past !

Nag   Tell off a horse !

Nappy   Liable to fall asleep in History lessons !

Narrow Minded   What you are when you have a splitting headache !

Near Miss   Avoid bullies by standing close to
the teacher !

Neck Line   Vampire's target !

Neptune   Song heard under water !

Nerve Cell   Where naughty nerves are kept in prison !

Nick Name   Steal someone's name !

Nightmare   Vampire horse !

Night School   Vampire college !

Nipper   Baby crab !

Numbskull	Very cold skeleton !
Nursery School	Where small plants go !

Oblique	The feeling you get at the start of a threehour maths exam !
Oblong	The feeling you get when you have finished all the questions and it is still only half way through a three hour maths exam !
Octopus	Cat born in October !
Odin	Noisy God !
Off Cut	Bad hairdo !
Offenbach	Noisy dog !

ALPHABET

Opportune	Music played on a pogo stick !
Optical	Tickle an opera singer !
Organ Grinder	Monster with food processor !
Out Of Bounds	Escaped from prison !
Outside Broadcast	Shout through window !
Overcast	Throw fishing rod into middle of river !
Overgrown	Too big for last year's blazer !

P

Paddock	Where horse ships dock !
Palatable	Tasty table for monsters to eat !
Paperweight	Heavy school bag !
Parapet	Pet parrot kept by parachutist !
Parity	Two parrots exactly the same !
Partial Eclipse	Half trimmed hedge !
Password	Hand a note to someone in class !
Pebble Dash	Running with a stone in your trainer !

Pedigree	Degree for posh dogs !
Perch	Fish kept in a cage !
Perspex	Plastic spectacles !
Phoney	Fake mobile phone !
Physiotherapy	Medicine mixed with lemonade !
Picador	Select an entrance to a bullfight !
Pigment	Paints for pigs !
Pigswill	How a dead pig leaves things to his family !
Pillar Box	What posties sleep on at night !
Ping - Pong	Table tennis played by skunks !

Pizzicato   Pizza for cats !

Plasma   Mum made by a plastic surgeon !

Plus Fours   Trousers worn by maths teachers !

Po faced   The way you are supposed to look reading serious poetry !

Pole Vault   Where the expensive poles are locked away !

Polygon   Missing parrot !

Polystyrene — Plastic parrot !

Pontoon — Song sung by card players !

Puddle — What you find on the pavement when it has been raining cats and dogs !

Punch Line — End of a boxing joke !

Quadruped — Bicycle with 4 pedals !

Quicksand — Sand that runs away when you're not looking !

Quicksilver — Money that's easy to spend !

Quiz master — Ask teacher questions he can't answer !

R

Rag and Bone Man Skeleton working in a clothes shop !

Rainbow Bow tie for a raindrop !

Raleigh Explorer who invented the bicycle !

Raspberry Very rude fruit !

Remorse Send coded signal again !

Reverse Charge Telephone to stop herd of Rhinos squashing you !

Road Hog Pig driving badly !

Rush Hour When bullrushes go home from work

Rustler	Woman in a tissue paper dress!

S

Sand Bank	Where camels keep their savings!
Sandpaper	Newspaper designed to be read on the beach!
Sapsucker	Vampire who likes fools!
Satire	Telling jokes sitting on a tall stool!

Saxophone	Saxon telephone !
Scotch Egg	What you get from chickens fed on whisky !
Scrap Book	List of fights you've been in !
Scullery	Monster's kitchen !
Sharp Witted	Someone with a pointed head !

Shop Lifter	King Kong !
Siesta	Car that never wakes up !

Skull Cap	What a skull boy wears !
Slip Road	Where it's icy enough to make a slide !
Snowball	Formal do for snowmen and women !
Solar Flares	Trousers worn at space discos !

Sour Puss	Cat that eats lemons !
Split Pea	Pea with a split personality !
Sponge Cake	What jellyfish eat at parties !
Stale Mate	Monster's friend !

ALPHABET

Staple Diet	Eating small bits of bent metal !
Steel Wool	What you get from robot sheep !
Stereotype	Type using two fingers !
Sticky Wicket	What bees leave after a cricket match !

T

Tadpole	What a tad uses in pole vaulting !
Tangent	Man who has been out in the sun !
Test Pilot	Someone who makes paper aeroplanes out of his test paper !
Three Legged Race	What monsters win on their own !
Time Machine	Space ship full of herbs !
Toadstools	What a toad mends his car with !
Transparent	Glass mum or dad !
Trunk Call	Telephone an elephant !
Tuck Shop	Where Robin Hood first met Friar Tuck !

Tuning Fork	To make sure your musical chairs are all in tune !

Undercover	Spy hidden under your duvet !
Unearth	When a vampire visits a friend !
Unlucky	Running into a vampire when you are trying to escape from a werewolf !
Unmentionables	Censored !!
Unplug	What you should do with an electric chair before you sit down !

V

Vaccination	A country where everyone has had a jab !

Vagabond	What you tie up a tramp with !
Vamoose	Run away from a ghostly elk !
Vampire Bat	What vampires play cricket with !
Vancouver	Garage !
Vulgar Fraction	A fraction with bad manners !

W

Watchdog   A dog that can tell the time !

Water Bed   Where crabs sleep !

Water Polo   What horses play in the swimming pool !

Water Table   Where fish eat their dinners !

Wear and Tear What oversized monsters do with
                   their clothes!

Weight Watcher Someone who looks at his tum in
                   the mirror all day long !

Wigwam   When your wig falls over your eyes and
                   you walk into a lamp post !

Witch Craft	Broomstick !
Wolf Whistle	What a fox referee uses !
Wonkey	Unsteady Donkey !
Wrap	Music for mummies !

X - Y - Z

Xylophone	What you use to telephone someone on the planet Xylo !
X-Ray	The ghost of Ray !

Yankee Doodle	American Cartoonist !
Yellow Lines	What you get if you misbehave at traffic warden school !
Yolks	Jokes told by chickens !
Youth Clubs	Cavemen's first weapon !
Zermatt	What you wipe zer feet on !
Zinc	Where you wash your face !
Zing	What you do with zongs in a choir !
Zoo	What a solicitor does !
Zoom Lens	The sound of a camera falling from a great height !
Zulu	The toilets in the zoo !

WHAT?

What do you call a scared biscuit ?

A Cowardy Custard Cream !

What do you call a man whose father was a Canon?

A son of a gun!

What do you call a man with two left feet?

Whatever you like - if he tries to catch you
he'll just run round in circles!

WHAT?

What do you call a
weekly television
programme about
people getting
washed ?

A soap opera !

What do you call a
flock of birds who
fly in formation ?

The Red Sparrows !

What do you call a bee who is always complaining ?

A Grumble Bee !

What would you call a friend who had an elephant
on his head ?

A Flatmate !

What do you call a posh pig delivering newspapers ?

Bacon Rind !

What do you call a teacher who makes fireworks ?

A Head Banger !

What do you call a man who drills holes in teapots ?

A Potholer !

What do you call a song played on car horns?

A Car Tune!

What do you call the man who invented a famous car and toilet paper?

Lou Rolls!

What do you call an elephant that has had too much to drink?

Trunk!

What do you call
the owner of a tool
factory ?

The Vice Chairman !

What do you call
King Midas when
he stars in a James
Bond film ?

Goldfinger !

What do you call a
parrot when it has
dried itself after a
bath ?

Polly Unsaturated !

What do you call a dentist in the army ?

A Drill Sergeant !

What do you call a Kangaroo at the North Pole ?

A Lost - Tralien !

What do you call a rabbit dressed up as a cake ?

A Cream Bun !

What do you call the man who went to a fancy dress party as a sandwich?

Roland Butter!

What do you call a man who rescues drowning spooks from the sea?

A Ghost Guard!

What do you call someone who makes half size models of fish?

A Scale Modeller!

What do you call someone who draws funny pictures of motor vehicles ?

A Car - Toonist !

What do you call someone who dances on cars ?

A Morris Dancer !

What do you call a fight between film actors ?

Star Wars !

What do you call a group of cars?

A Clutch!

What do you call a puzzle that is so hard it makes people swear?

A Crossword!

What do you call a dog that is always getting into fights?

A Boxer!

What do you call a witch's broomstick when you are very young?

A Broom Broom!

What do you call a film about Mallards?

A Duckumentary!

What do you call a musical instrument that is played by two teams of twenty people?

A Piano Forte!

What do you call a very fast horse ?

Gee Gee Whizz !

What do you call the best dad in the world ?

Top of the Pops !

What do you call a chocolate that teases small animals ?

A Mole - teaser !

What do you call a fish on a motorcycle ?

A Motor Pike !

What do you call a pen with no hair ?

A Bald Point !

What do you call a thing with 22 legs,
11 heads and 2 wings ?

A Football Team !

What do you call a cow that cuts grass ?

A Lawn Mooooper !

What do you call a magical secret agent?

James Wand!

What do you call it when an aeroplane
disappears over the horizon?

Boeing, Going, Gone!

What do you call a hearing aid made from fruit?

A Lemonade!

PARDON??

What do you call a policeman with blonde hair ?

A Fair Cop !

What do you call a 5-a-side match played
by chimney sweeps ?

Soot Ball !

What do you call a small parent ?

A Minimum !

What do you call a traffic warden who never fines anyone ?

A Triffic Warden !

What do you call a telephone call from one vicar to another ?

A Parson to Parson call !

What do you call the place where parrots make films ?

PollyWood !

What do you call a scared biscuit ?

A Cowardy Custard Cream !

What do you call an Igloo without a toilet ?

An Ig !

What do you call a superb painting done
by a rat ?

A Mouseterpiece !

What do you call a box of parrot food ?

Polly Filla !

What do you call it when you pass out after
eating too much curry ?

A Korma !

What do you call a chicken that eats cement ?

A Bricklayer !

What do you get if you cross a toad
with a science fiction film ?

Star warts !

What do you get if you cross a road
with a blindfold ?

Knocked down !

What do you get if you cross a mouse
with a tin opener ?

Something that can get the cheese from the
'fridge without even opening the door !

What do you get if you cross a car with
the millenium ?

A Rover 2000 !

What do you get if you cross a
bridge with your feet ?

To the other side !

What do you get if you cross a parrot
and a scary film ?

A bad attack of the polly-wobbles !

What do you get if you cross a car
with a row of mountains ?

A Range Rover !

What do you get if you cross a wizard
and an aeroplane ?

A flying sorcerer !

What do you get if you cross a
plant pot and an infant ?

A growing child !

What do you get if you cross a
football team and a pig ?

Queens Pork Rangers !

What do you get if you cross a hive of bees with a
jumper knitting pattern ?

Nice and swarm !

What do you get if you cross a
fish and a deaf person ?

A herring aid !

What do you get if you cross two vicars
and a telephone line ?

A parson to parson call !

What do you get if you cross a
computer with a beefburger ?

A big mac !

What do you get if you cross a
rhinocerous with a cat ?

Very worried mice !

What do you get if you cross a sheep
with a steel bar ?

Wire wool !

What dc you get if you cross a sheep
with an octopus ?

Jumpers with eight arms !

What do you get if you cross a sheep
with a plant ?

Cotton wool !

What do you get if you cross a sheep
with an outboard motor !

Baa Baa Baa Baa Baa Baa Baa Baa Baa Baa Baa Baa..

What do you get if you cross a dog
with a vegetable ?

A Jack Brussel terrier !

What do you get if you cross a sheep with a pub ?

A cocktail Baaa !

What do you get if you cross a
comedy author with a ghost ?

A crypt writer !

What do you get if you cross two
skeletons and an argument ?

A bone of contention !

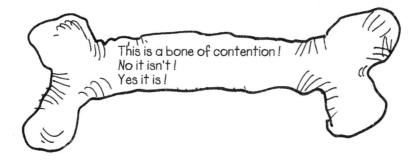

This is a bone of contention !
No it isn't !
Yes it is !

What do you get if you cross a witch and a
bowl of breakfast cereal ?

Snap, cackle and pop !

What do you get if you cross a spinach eater,
a suitmaker and a hippy ?

Popeye the tailor, man !

What do you get if you cross a coat and a fire ?

A blazer !

What do you get if you cross a shark
and Father Christmas ?

Santa jaws !

What do you get if you cross a waiter
and a slippery floor ?

Flying suacers !

What do you get if you cross a tropical
fruit and a sad dog ?

A melon collie !

What do you get if you cross a
baby and a snake ?

A rattler !

What do you get if you cross
a chicken with a kangaroo ?

Pouched eggs !

What do you get if you cross a penguin
with a hungry schoolchild ?

An empty wrapper !

What do you get if you cross a donkey with a mole ?

Mule hills in your garden !

What do you get if you cross a Star Wars
robot with a sheep ?

R 2 D ewe !

What do you get if you cross a chicken
with a cement lorry ?

A bricklayer !

What do you get if you cross a monster and
a bowl of breakfast cereal ?

Dreaded wheat !

What do you get if you cross a bad golfer and an outboard motor ?

Putt putt putt putt putt putt putt putt putt...

What do you get if you cross a track suit and a tortoise ?

A shell suit !

What do you get if you cross a cat with a cushion ?

A cat a pillow !

What do you get if you cross a skeleton and a supermodel ?

Not an ounce of fat !

What do you get if you cross a Prime Minister and a bunny ?

Blair Rabbit !

What do you get if you cross a Prime Minister
and a pair of grimy spectacles ?

Blaired vision !

What do you get if you cross a great
invention with a herb ?

A thyme machine !

What do you get if you cross a parking
space and a camel ?

A camelot!

What do you get if you cross an
alien with a pair of gloves ?

Green fingers !

What do you get if you cross a sore throat
and some Christmas decorations ?

Tinselitis !

What do you get if you cross a half
open door and a queue of cars ?

Ajar of jam !

What do you get if you cross a turkey
with an octopus ?

A leg for everyone at Christmas dinner !

What do you get if you cross China
with a car horn ?

Hong King !

What do you get if you cross a bed with
a set of cricket wickets ?

A three poster !

What do you get if you cross a hat
with a mountain top ?

A peaked cap !

What do you get if you cross a
vegetable with a 26 mile run ?

A Marrow - thon !

What do you get if you cross a rodent and someone who cleans your home ?

A mousekeeper !

What do you get if you cross a ghost and a Christmas play ?

A Phantomime !

What do you get if you cross a television personality and a jungle animal ?

A Gnus reader !

What do you get if you cross a stick insect
and a TV presenter ?

Stickolas Parsons !

What do you get if you cross a golf club
and a burrowing animal ?

A mole in one !

What do you get if you cross a cow with a pillar box ?

Postman cow pat !

What do you get if you cross a joke book
with an Oxo cube ?

A laughing stock !

What do you get if you cross a surgeon
and an octopus ?

A doctorpus !

What do you get if you cross a robot
with a drinks machine ?

C - tea - P - O !

What do you get if you cross a playing card
with a fizzy drink ?

Joker cola !

What do you get if you cross a robot with a foot ?

C - 3 - P - toe !

What do you get if you cross a
day of the week with buuble gum ?

Chewsday !

What do you get if you cross vampires
with some cheddar ?

Bancheese !

What do you get if you drop an iron
on someone's head?

Hard water!

What do you get if you cross an
octopus with a fountain pen?

A squidgy pen with 8 nibs that
makes all its own ink!

What do you get if you cross a horse with a
cake and a long rubber strip ?

A bun - gee - gee jumper !

What do you get if you cross a centipede
with a children's toy ?

A lego, lego, lego, lego, lego, lego,..............
.lego, lego, lego, set

What do you get if you cross a laundry basket
with a shopping basket ?

Man eating underpants !

What do you get if you cross a fairy and a turkey ?

A very strange Goblin !

What do you get if you cross a joke book
and two dozen eggs ?

A book with at least 24 yolks in it !

What do you get if you cross a fish
with a modelmaker ?

A scale model !

What do you get if you cross milk, fruit
and a scary film ?

A strawberry milk shake !

What do you get if you cross a mountain
with hiccups ?

A volcano !

What athlete do you get if you cross
a snake and a sheep ?

A long jumper !

What do you get if you cross an ant and a calculator ?

An account - ant !

What do you get if you cross a pig
and a very old radio ?

Lots of crackling !

What do you get if you cross a
cricket ball and an alien ?

A bowling green !

What do you get if you cross a tall
building and a home for pigs ?

A sty - scraper !

What do you get if you cross an army
and some babies ?

The infantry !

What do you get if you cross a breadcake
and a cattle rustler ?

A beef burglar !

What do you get if you cross a window
and a shirt collar ?

A pane in the neck !

What do you get if you cross a
can of oil and a mouse ?

I don't know, but at least it doesn't sqeak !

What do you get if you cross a sheep
with a discount store ?

Lots of baaaaagains !

What do you get if you
cross a holidaymaker
and an elephant ?

**Something that carries
its own trunk !**

What do you get if you
cross a camel and a
ghost ?

**Something that goes
hump in the night !**

What do you get if you cross a ghost
and a pair
of glasses ?

Spook - tacles !

What do you get if you cross a fox
with a policeman ?

A brush with the law !

What do you get if you cross a
jewellers shop with a boxer ?

A window full of boxing rings !
What do you get if you cross a feather
with a carnation ?

Tickled pink !

What do you get if you cross a spider
with a football ground ?

Webley stadium !

What do you get if you cross a boy band and some bottles of lemonade ?

A pop group !

What do you get if you cross a toad with someone who tells strange jokes ?

Someone with a wart sense of humour !

What do you get if you cross a crying baby and a football fan ?

A footbawler !

What do you get if you cross a chimpanzee
with an oven ?

A hairy griller !

What do you get if you cross an oil well
with bad manners ?

Crude oil !

What do you get if you cross electricity
and a chicken ?

Battery eggs !

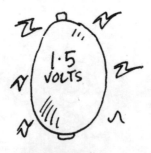

What do you get if you cross a fish and a birdcage ?

Perch !

What do you get if you cross a
butcher and a dance ?

A meatball !

What do you get if you cross
a scratch on your arm
and a fruit ?

A lemon sore - bit !

ONCH

What do you get if you cross a skunk
and a winning lottery ticket ?

Stinking rich !

What do you get if you cross a ball
and a blunt instrument ?

A football club !

What do you get if you cross the sea
and a pot of chilli ?

A Mexican wave !

What do you get if you cross a donkey and a three legged milking stool ?

A wonkey !

What do you get if you cross a sheep and an ink cartridge ?

Something that only a sheepdog can get into a pen !

What do you get if you cross a lawn and a mattress ?

A flower bed !

What do you get if you cross a...
cat with a set of water colours ?

Pusster Paints !

What do you get if you cross a...
dog and an elephant ?

No more post !

What do you get if you cross a...
giraffe and a dog ?

**Something that bites the tyres of low
flying aircraft !**

What do you get if you cross a...
range of mountains with a dancer ?

Something huge dancing peak to peak !

What do you get if you cross a...
penguin with a paratrooper ?

A chocolate soldier !

What do you get if you cross a...
cartoon with some bubble gum ?

A carica - chewer !

What do you get if you cross a...
fox and a policeman ?

A brush with the law !

What do you get if you cross a...
postman, his pet cat and a field of cows ?

Postman pat and his black and white cow pat !

What do you get if you cross a...
pencil with window covers ?

Blinds that draw themselves !

What do you get if you cross a...
pig and a flea ?

Pork scratchings !

What do you get if you cross a...
Welshman and a saint ?

Good Evans !

What do you get if you cross a...
bottle of pop and a frog ?

Croaka Cola !

What do you get if you cross a...
budgie and a clown ?

Cheep and cheerful !

What do you get if you cross a...
comedian, an owl and a tube of adhesive ?

A Wit Who Glues !

What do you get if you...
pinch part of an elderly Scotsman's fish supper ?

A chip off the old Jock !

What do you get if you cross a...
field of cows and a motor boat ?

Pat pat pat pat pat pat pat pat pat.....

BRAINTEASERS

Why did the hen cross the road?

To prove she wasn't chicken!

What do you call a man with a tree growing
out of his head?

Ed - Wood !

How do you stop a head cold going to your chest?

Easy - tie a knot in your neck!

Why shouldn't you try to swim on a full stomach?

Because it's easier to swim on a full swimming pool!

What creature sticks to the bottom of sheep ships?

Baaa - nacles!

How do you know if your little brother is turning into a 'fridge ?

See if a little light comes on whenever he opens his mouth !

What is the coldest part of the North Pole ?

An explorer's nose !

What do computer operators eat for lunch ?

Chips !

Why is that man standing in the sink ?

He's a tap dancer !

Where do rabbits learn to fly ?

In the Hare Force !

How did the witch know she was getting better ?

Because the doctor let her get
out of bed for a spell !

BRAINTEASERS

What did the witch call her baby daughter ?

Wanda !

How do witch children listen to stories ?

Spellbound !

'Which witch went to Ipswich ?
The rich witch called little Mitch,
with the light switch for the soccer pitch,
who twitched and fell in a ditch;
that witch went to Ipswich -
and never came home !

What would you find in a rabbit's library?

Bucks!

Why can you never swindle a snake?

Because it's impossible to pull its leg!

What did the overweight ballet dancer perform?

The dance of the sugar plump fairy!

Why is it easy to swindle a sheep ?

Because it is so easy to pull the wool over its eyes !

What do elves eat at parties ?

Fairy Cakes !

What do you get if you cross a brain surgeon
and a herd of cows ?

Cow-operation !

Why did the carpenter go to the doctor ?

He had a saw hand !

What is the only true cure for dandruff ?

Baldness !

What should you buy if your hair falls out ?

A good vacuum cleaner !

A man went to see his doctor with a brick buried in his head. What was he suffering from ?

Falling arches !

BRAINTEASERS

Why did the doctor operate on the man who swallowed a pink biro ?

He had a cute-pen-inside-is !

Nurse - why are you putting Mr Smith's left leg in plaster, it's his right leg that's broken ?!

It's OK, I'm new so I'm practising on the left one first to make sure I do it properly!

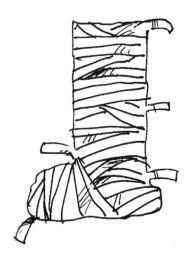

What sort of fish would you find in a bird cage ?

A Perch !

What sort of fish would you find in a shoe ?

An Eel !

What sort of dance do fish do at parties ?

The Conga !

Where did the dog breeder keep his savings ?

In bark-lays bank !

Did you hear about the bungee jumper who shot up and down for 3 hours before they could bring him under control ?

He had a yo-yo in his pocket !

What do you call a cowboy who helps out in a school?

The Deputy Head!

What do you call the teacher in the school who gives out forms that you have to fill in?

The Form Teacher!

Did you hear about the dog who was arrested?

He didn't pay a barking ticket!

Where did the rich cat live ?

In a mews cottage !

What position did the witch play in the football team ?

Sweeper !

What position did the pile of wood play in
the football team ?

De-fence !

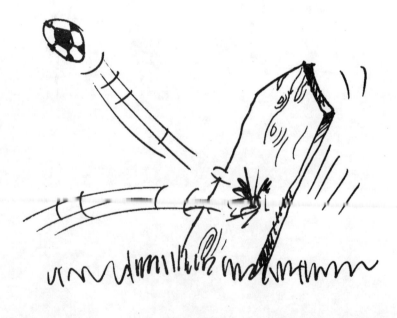

Why couldn't the slow boxer get a drink at the party?

Because everyone beat him to the punch!

Why was the archaeologist upset?

His job was in ruins!

Why was the butcher worried?

His job was at steak!

Why did the teacher have to turn the lights on ?

Because his pupils were so dim !

Why did the French farmer only keep the one chicken ?

Because in France one egg is un oeuf !

What did the farmer say when all his cows
charged him at once ?

I'm on the horns of a dilemma here !

What sort of snake will tell on you ?
A grass snake !

Why did the doll blush ?

Because she saw the Teddy Bear !

POINTLESS INVENTIONS...

Camouflage for stick insects !

Disposable rubbish bags !

Colour radio !

Invisible traffic lights !

Plastic tea bags !

Waterproof soap !

Fireproof petrol !

WHERE ARE THE DISPOSABLE RUBBISH BAGS ?

I'VE THROWN THEM AWAY

What sort of ring is always square ?

A boxing ring !

What sort of queue is always straight ?

A snooker cue !

What sort of net is useless for catching fish ?

A football net !

BRAINTEASERS

Why do people leave letters at the football ground?

They want to catch the last goal-post!

I've got a terrible fat belly!

Have you tried to diet?

Yes, but whatever colour I use it still looks fat!

What do you call a frog that helps children safely across the street?

The green cross toad!

Did you hear about the posh chef with an attitude problem?

He had a french fried potato on his shoulder!

Why do golfers carry a spare sock?

Because they might get a hole in one!

A rather dim gardener from Leeds,
once swallowed a packet of seeds.
In just a few weeks,
his ears turned to leeks,
and his hair was a tangle of weeds!

I once met a man from Hong Kong,
who'd been jogging for twenty years long.
He was terribly sweaty,
– he looked like a yeti,
and his feet had a terrible pong!

BRAINTEASERS

What book do you buy to teach children
how to fight ?

A scrapbook !

What sort of animals make the best TV presenters ?

Gnus - readers !

What sort of animal is best at getting up
in the morning ?

A LLama clock !

I hear you've just invented gunpowder ?

Yes, I was using some candles to light my laboratory and it came to me in a flash !

How is your other invention coming along – you know, the matches ?

Oh ! They've been a striking success !

Why did the doctor take his nose to pieces ?

He wanted to see what made it run !

Why is it dangerous to tell jokes to Humpty Dumpty ?

He might crack up !

Blenkinsop - stop acting the fool -
I'm in charge of this class, not you !

Why do pens get sent to prison ?

To do long sentences !

What was the parrot doing in prison ?

It was a jail-bird !

What is the name of the detective who sings quietly to himself while solving crimes?

Sherlock Hums!

Why did the farmer feed his pigs sugar and vinegar?

He wanted sweet and sour pork!

What do you call the Scottish dentist?

Phil McCavity!

Why is the soil in my garden always dry?

Because you have leeks!

What kind of rose
has a bark ?

A dog rose !

What did the little
boy say when he
wanted his big
brother to give him
back his building
bricks ?

Lego !

Why are you called
Postman Pat ?

**Because I have to
deliver post to all
the farms !**

Which two words
in the English
language have the
most letters ?

Post Office !

How do you start a jelly baby race ?

Ready - Set - Go !

What sort of music was invented by fish ?

Sole music !

What gets smaller the more you put in it ?

A hole in the ground !

BRAINTEASERS

Waiter, why is there a dead fly in my soup?

Well, you surely don't expect to get
a live one at these prices!

What happened to the man who
stole a lorry load of eggs?

He gave himself up - he said he only did it for a yolk!

Stop! This is a one-way street!

Well, I'm only going one way !?

Yes, but everyone else is going the other way!

Well, you're a policeman, make them turn round!

What is the thing that is most red at Christmas?

Rudolph's nose!

How do penguins get to school ?

On 21 speed mountain icicles !

Why do cows have horns ?

Because they would look pretty silly
with bells on their heads !

Mary had a little lamb,
which she dressed in pretty blouses,
she also had a ferret,
which she put down her dad's trousers !

What goes MOOOOOZ ?
A jet flying backwards !

What do blacksmiths eat for breakfast ?

Vice Crispies !

Why do toolmakers always escape from fires ?

They know the drill !

What self defence method do mice use ?

Ka - rat - e !

What did the stupid burglar do when he saw
a 'WANTED' poster outside the police station ?

He went in and applied for the job !

What is a big game hunter ?

Someone who can't find the football stadium !

BRAINTEASERS

30 people were sheltering under an umbrella,
how many of them got wet?

None - it wasn't raining!

Why are burglars such good tennis players?

**Because they spend such a lot of their time
in courts!**

Is that a new perfume I smell?

It is, and you do!

What do vampires use to 'phone relatives?

A terror - phone!

What are wasps favourite flowers?

Bee - gonias!

BRAINTEASERS

Why did the fly fly ?

Because the spider spied her !

What sort of monster is musical ?

The one with A Flat head !

Where do Chinese vampires live ?

Fang - Hai !

Why did the Romans build straight roads ?

They didn't want anyone hiding round the corners !

What do you call a dinosaur that
keeps you awake at night?

Bronto - snore - us !

What is the name of the Australian dog drummer ?

Dingo Starr !

Why have you buried my car ?

Because the battery is dead !

What did the bull say when he came back
from the china shop ?

I've had a really smashing time !

When do 2 and 2 make more than 4 ?

When they make 22 !

Why were the naughty eggs sent out of the class ?

For playing practical yolks !

Why should you never listen too closely to the match ?

Because you might burn your ears !

BRAINTEASERS

Why did the bakers work late ?

Because they kneaded the dough !

How many monsters would it take to fill this room ?

No idea, I'd be off after the first one arrived !

How does Father Christmas start a joke ?

This one will sleigh you...!

What jewelry do ghosts wear ?

Tombstones !

What do mummies use to wash up ?

Pharaoh liquid !

How can you sleep like a log ?

Put your bed in the fireplace !

What do space monster sweet shops sell ?

Mars bars, galaxy and milky way !

What can you catch and hold but never touch ?

Your breath !

What do you call the finest Indian wine ?

Vin - daloo !

What are dog biscuits made from ?

Collie - flour !

What flower do you have to keep a look out for in the garden ?

Anenome !

Where would you find secret soup ?

At the minestrone of defence !

SECRET SOUP

007 VARIETIES

KEEP OUT !

What do you do if a ghoul rolls his eyes at you ?

Just pick them up and roll them back !

Why did the man jump up and down
after taking his medicine ?

Because he forgot to shake the bottle
before he took it !

Which famous
artist had a bad
cold ?

Vincent van
cough !

Why did the
burglar buy a
surf board ?

He wanted to
start a crime
wave !

What does a toad sit on ?

A toadstool !

What does a toad use for making furniture ?

A toad's tool !

Why don't pigs telephone one another ?

Because there is too much crackling on the line !

Why are pigs no good at do-it-yourself ?

Because they are ham-fisted !

Why did the burglar break into the music shop ?

He was after the lute !

Why did the burglar break into the bakers ?

He wanted to steal the dough !

BRAINTEASERS

Why did the burglar go to the bank ?

To recycle his bottles !

How do you keep a fool in suspense ?

I'll tell you tomorrow !

How do you make a fool laugh on Saturday ?

Tell him a joke on Wednesday !

Why must you never make a
noise in a hospital ?

Because you don't want to
wake the sleeping pills !

What is a squirrel's favourite
chocolate ?

Whole nut !

Where would you find a bee ?

At the start of the alphabet !

Where is there always a queue ?

In between P and R !

What does it mean if your nose starts to run ?

It's trying to catch a cold !

Why is the Leopard the only animal that can't
hide from hunters ?

Because it is always spotted !

Why did the elephant refuse to play cards
with his two friends ?

**Because one of them was lion and
the other was a cheetah !**

How do you make a Venetian blind ?

Paint his spectacles black when he's asleep !

Who is a caveman's favourite band ?

The stones !

Why does a giraffe have such a long neck ?

Have you ever smelled a giraffe's feet !

Mary had a little fox,
it ate her little goat,
now everywhere that Mary goes,
she wears her fox-skin coat !

What jungle animal would you find at the North Pole ?

A lost one !

BRAINTEASERS

What sort of frog is covered in dots and dashes ?

A morse toad !

Where do cows go for history lessons ?

To a mooseum !

What does a polar bear use to keep his head warm ?

A polar ice cap !

What does a hard of hearing apple have in his ear ?

A lemonade !

How do plumbers get to work ?

By tube !

I'LL BE THERE IN TEN MINUTES

What sort of music do police officers like ?

Anything with a regular boat !

BRAINTEASERS

What do you need to electrocute
an orchestra ?

A good conductor !

Good morning Mr Butcher, do you have pig's feet ?

Certainly, sir !

Well, wear larger shoes and no-one will notice !

How do teddies like to ride horses ?

Bear back !

What do teddies take when they are
going on holiday ?

Just the bear essentials !

Waiter, there's a small worm in my salad !

Oh, dear, I'll tell the chef to send you a large one !

Who always puts thyme in his soup ?

A clockmender !

What do you give a dog for breakfast ?

Pooched eggs !

Why couldn't the orange call the apple on the telephone ?

Because the lime was engaged !

Why are those clothes running out of the sports shop ?

They're jogging suits !

Why do video machines always win their football matches ?

Because they have fast forwards !

What sort of fruit would you find in a diary ?

Dates !

Why do cows lie down together when it rains ?

To keep each udder dry !

What do vegetarians take home for wages ?

A Celery !

Atissshhhooo, I don't feel very well !

Wow, I didn't know that having a cold affected
your sense of touch !

BRAINTEASERS

Did you hear about the punk rocker who fell over and 50 others fell over at the same time ?

He started a chain reaction !

What do you call a man who never pays his bills ?

Owen !

What do mice sing at birthday parties ?

For cheese a jolly good fellow !

When should you put your electric guitar in the fridge ?

When you want to play some really cool music !

Where is the greenest city in Europe ?

Brussels !

Which Italian city is good for wandering round ?

Rome !

Which English city has the best stock of electrical connectors ?

Leeds !

Which French city has the best stock of paper ?

Rheims !

Why are bearded men fearless ?

Because they can never have a close shave !

What song do sweets sing at parties ?

For he's a jelly good fellow !

How do you write a essay on a giraffe ?

With a long ladder !

How do you shock people at a tea party ?

Serve currant buns !

What says 'now you see me, now you don't...'

A nun on a zebra crossing !

Why do vampires like crossword puzzles ?

They like the crypt - ic clues !

My cellar is full of toadstools !

How do you know they're toadstools ?

There's not mushroom in there for anything else !

Why do some anglers suck their maggots ?

So they can wait for a fish to bite with baited breath !

BRAINTEASERS

Should I give the dog some of my pie?

Certainly not, he didn't want it when I gave it to him earlier!

What shampoo do spooks use?

Wash - n - ghost!

What sort of ghosts haunt hospitals?

Surgical spirits!

What do you get if you cross a skunk with an owl?

Something that stinks, but doesn't give a hoot!

How do you tell a ghost
how lovely they are ?

'you're bootiful !'

What did the doctor give
Cleopatra for her
headache ?

An asp - irin !

What do you give a
ghost with a headache ?

AAAAGGGGHHHHspirin !

Where do vampires go on holiday ?

Veinice !

How do you know if a bicycle is haunted ?

Look for spooks in the wheels !

What do you call a doctor with a bright green stethoscope ?

Doctor !

What sort of parties do vampires like best ?

Fang - cy dress parties !

Why should you never tell your secrets to a piglet ?

Because they might squeal !

How do rabbits go on holiday ?

By British hareways !

How do you talk to a hen ?

By using fowl language !

Who is the patron saint of toys ?

Saint Francis of a see-saw !

Which teacher won't allow sick notes ?

The music teacher !

What is a *juggernaut* ?

An empty jug !

What does B.C. stand for ?

Before calculators !

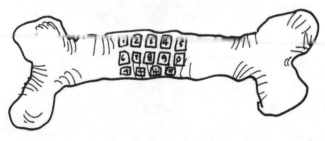

What did the stupid fencing team take to the olympics ?

5000 litres of creosote !

Which trees grow at the seaside ?

Beach trees !

How do you make a Mexican chilli ?

Take him to Iceland !

What do cannibals do at a wedding ?

They toast the bridge and groom !

What is a mistake ?

An unmarried female bank robber !

Why is the bookshop the tallest
building in the town ?

Because it has the
most stories !

Who do you ask to see if you
find a twig in your salad ?

The branch manager !

What sort of person gets paid
to make faces all day ?

A clockmaker !

BRAINTEASERS

What happened when the vampire went insane ?

He went batty !

What sort of tree grows near a volcano ?

A lava tree !

What did the skunk say when the wind
changed direction ?

It's all coming back to me now !

Where do you find monster snails ?

On the end of monsters' fingers !

Why must you always have holes in your socks ?

You wouldn't be able to get your feet
in them if you didn't !

In which battle was Alexander the Great killed ?

His last one !

What is yellow, wears glasses and sings ?

'Nana Mouskouri !

BRAINTEASERS

In which film does fruit rule the world?

Planet of the grapes!

Where do squirrels keep their nuts?

In a pan-tree!

Which is the strongest day of the week?

Sunday - all the others are weak days!

What do you call someone who can't
stop stealing carpets?

A rug addict!

Which of these is correct -
'egg yolk is white'
'egg yolk are white'

Neither - egg yolk is yellow !

Where would you find a rubber trumpet ?

In an elastic band !

What goes up but never comes down ?

Your age !

Which birds fly in formation?

The Red Sparrows!

What do you call a lion with no eyes?

Lon!

Why are cars rubbish at football?

They only have one boot each!

Why did the satsuma go to the doctor ?

It wasn't peeling too good !

What music does King Neptune like ?

Sole !

Why does it snow in the Winter ?

Because it's too hot in the Summer !

BRAINTEASERS

What do you call a very old Dracula ?

Gran pire !

What sort of fish would you find in a bird cage ?

A perch !

What do you throw for a stick insect to fetch ?

A dog !

What is a vampires favourite coffee ?

Decoffinated !

Where do insects go to dance ?

A cricket ball !

Why is it impossible to open a locked piano lid ?

Because all the keys are on the inside !

What do you get if you read the Monster Kids'
Joke Book to an Oxo cube ?

A laughing stock !

What runs all the way round your house
without moving ?

The fence !

What show do undertakers look forward to every year ?

The hearse of the year show !

How do you measure the size of fruit ?

With a green gauge !

What do you get if you leave your
teaspoon in the cup ?

A sharp pain in the eye when you drink !

What has no legs, but runs across
the bathroom floor?

Water!

Why was the blacksmith arrested?

For forging!

What is it called when a fish tells lies in a courtroom?

Perchery!

Why is a bad bank like a lazy schoolboy ?

They both lose interest quickly !

What should you take if you feel run down ?

The number of the car that hit you !

Which robot was stuck in road works ?

R 2 Detour !

How do hens dance ?

Chick to chick !

Did you hear about the Martian who went to a
plastic surgeon for a face lift ? She wanted her
face to look like a million dollars, so the surgeon
made it all green and crinkly !

BRAINTEASERS

Where do Martians live ?

In greenhouses !

What do you give the man who has everything ?

Nothing !

Where would you
keep sheep covered
in ink ?

In a pen !

What do you call a story that someone
tells you at breakfast every day ?

A cereal !

What do you call a story that someone tells you
in the car on the way to school every day ?

A mini-serial !

BRAINTEASERS

Who drives her children to school in a small car ?

A minimum !

What do vampires do before driving a car ?

They check the wing mirrors !

Why do vampires never marry ?

They are bat - chelors !

Why do woodworm have no friends ?

Because they are boring creatures !

Where can you go for a quick break by the beach ?

A seaside karate club !

How do you stop your nose from running ?

Take away its trainers !

What is the best thing to put in a sandwich ?

Your teeth !

Who writes joke books in never never land !

Peter Pun !

BRAINTEASERS

What do you get if you cut a comedian in two ?

A half wit !

What do you get if you cross a bee with an ape ?

Sting Kong !

How do jockeys send messages to each other ?

With horse code !

What do dogs go to the hairdresser for ?

A shampoodle and setter !

What do they pay police officers for working late ?

Copper Nitrate !

Why did the cow look into the crystal ball ?

To see if there was a message from the udder side !

What did the doctor give the deaf fisherman ?

A herring aid !

Who thought up the
series 'Star Trek' ?

Some bright Spock !

Why couldn't the astronauts land on the moon ?

Because it was full !

What time is it when astronauts are hungry ?

Launch time !

How can you cook turkey that really tickles the taste buds ?

Leave the feathers on !

What's the special offer at the pet shop this week ?

Buy one cat - get one flea !

What do you call a bike that bites your bottom
when you try to get on it ?

A vicious cycle !

Why do demons and ghouls get on so well together ?

Because demons are a ghouls best friend !

What tool do ghostly builders use ?

A spirit level !

Why are lots of famous artists French ?

Because they were born in France !

NAMES

What do you call a man who owns a seaside
sweet factory?

Rock!

What do you call a man with a sack, a long white beard
and a sleigh ?

Bjorn, the oldest
postman in Iceland !

What do you call a monkey who is King of the jungle ?

Henry the Ape !

What do you call a woman with a shotgun in her hand ?

Whatever she tells you to, or else !

What do you call a woman who laughs as
she drives her car ?

Minnie Ha Ha !

What do you call a glove puppet
that sweeps chimneys ?

Sooty !

What name do you give a dog
that likes to wander off all the time ?

Rover !

What do you call a man who owns a seaside sweet
factory ?

Rock !

What do you call a woman with a frog on her head ?

Lily !

What do you call a man who lives in Scotland?

Glen!

What do you call the Roman Emperor who kept pet mice?

Julius Cheeser!

What do you call a man with a horse's head?

Nathan!

What do you call a woman who sells parrots?

Polly!

What do you call a woman who was eaten
by her cannibal husband?

Henrietta!

What was the name of the man who designed King
Arthur's round table?

Sir Cumference!

What do you call a man with a
car number plate on his head?

Reg!

What do you call a man with his head in the oven ?

Stew !

What do you call an Ancient Egyptian
with no teeth ?

A Gummy Mummy !

What do you call a man with a tissue paper head ?

Russell !

What do you call a man with a
speedometer
on his head ?

Miles !

What do you call a failed lion tamer ?

Claude Bottom !

What do you call a frightened man?

Hugo First!

What do you call a man with a bowl of porridge on his head?

Scott!

What do you call a man with an oil well on his head?

Derek!

What do you call a girl with a bag of chips ?

Anita !

What do you call a woman with a plant pot on her head ?

Rose !

What do you call a man who lifts
cars up in a garage ?

Jack !

What do you call a woman
who keeps horses ?

GiGi !

What do you call a man with
very strong spectacles ?

Seymore !

What do you call a man who dances with
bells round his ankles ?

Maurice !

What do you call a woman with a
cash register on her head ?

Tilly !

What do you call a man with a
stolen safe on his head?

Robin Banks!

What do you call a dog that is a always
rushing about?

A dash-hound!

What do you call a rodent that likes to sword fence?

A Mouseketeer!

What do you call a man who delivers
Christmas presents to lions and tigers?

Santa Claws!

What do you call a man who doesn't sink?

Bob!

What do you call a woman who knows
where she lives?

Olivia!

What do you call the super heroes
who got run over ?

Flatman and Ribbon !

What do you call the illness that martial
arts experts catch ?

Kung Flu !

What do you call a man with a
computer on his head ?

Mac !

What do you call a man with a
duck on his head ?

Donald !

What do you call a woman who
works at the zoo ?

Ellie Fant !

NAMES

What do you call a man with
horses on his head ?

Jim Karna !

What do you call a woman with a ball of
wool on her head ?

Barbara Black Sheep !

What did the Spaniard call his first
and only son ?

Juan !

What do you call a man with a vaulting horse
on his head ?

Jim !

What do you call a girl who comes out
very early in the morning ?

Dawn !

What do you call a girl with
cakes on her head ?

Bunty !

What do you call a man with money on his head ?

Bill !

What do you call a boy with an
arm and a leg on his head ?

Hand - toe - knee !

What do you call a man with a small pig on his head ?

Hamlet !

What do you call a man with a male cat on his head ?

Tom !

What do you call a woman who plays snooker with a pint of beer on her head?

Beatrix Potter!

What do you call a man with a castle on his head?

Fort William!

What do you call a man with a box of treasure on his head?

Chester!

What do you call a woman with a
sinking ship on her head?

Mandy Lifeboats!

What do you call a woman with a
pyramid on her head?

Mummy!

What do you call a man with a
police car on his head?

Nick, nick, nick...!

What do you call a man with
a wooden head?

Edward!

What do you call a woman with
two toilets on her head ?

Lulu !

What do you call a girl with a
head made of sugar ?

Candy !

What do you call a girl with
a head made of glass ?

Crystal !

What do you call a girl with a
head made of honey ?

Bee - trix !

What do you call a man with
legal documents on his head ?

Will !

What do you call a man with a steering wheel and gearstick on his head?

Morris!

And what do you call his son?

Morris Minor!

What do you call a woman with a tub of butter on her head?

Marge!

What do you call a lion with toothache?

Rory!

What do you call a man with a jumbo jet parked on his head?

Ron Way!

What do you call a man with an anvil on his head?

Smith!

What do you call a woman with
a boat tied up to her head?

Maude!

What do you call a man with a
heavy good vehicle on his head?

Laurie!

What do you call a dog that's
always snapping at people?

Camera!

What do you call a criminal with
a fish down his trousers?

The Codfather!

What do you call a girl with a
bucket and spade on her head?

Sandy!

What do you call a girl with an
orange on her head ?

Clementine !

What do you call a girl with a chimney
on her head ?

Ruth !

What do you call a man with
a pile of hay on his head ?

Rick !

What do you call a man with
turf on his head ?

Pete !

What do you call a man with a school
register on his head ?

Mark !

What do you call a girl with flowers
growing out of her head?

Daisy!

(The girl with the beauty spot!)

What do you call a man with a
vegetable patch
on his head?

Mr Bean!

What do you call a woman with a
badly fitted head ?

Lucy !

What do you call a play acted by ghosts ?

A Phantomime !

What do you call a Scottish lunchtime assistant ?

Dinner Ken !

What do you call the ghost that
haunts TV chat shows ?

The Phantom of the Oprah !

What do you call a man with a
road map on his head ?

Miles !

What do you call a woman with a kettle on her head ?

Polly !

(well, in the nursery rhyme
Polly put the kettle on ?!)

What do you a man with a pair of
spectacles on his head ?

Luke !

What do you call a woman with a
doll on her head ?

Sindy !

What do you call a man with a
sprig of holly on his head ?

Buddy !

What do you call a man with a large
fiery planet on his head ?

Sunny !

What do you call a woman with some
thin paper and a pencil on her head ?

Tracey !

What do you call a woman with
half a lizard on her head?

Liz!

What do you call a man with a used
postage stamp on his head?

Frank!

What do you call a man with a policeman on his head?

Bobby!

What do you call a woman with a plate of
food on her head?

Amelia!

What do you call a vampire with
a calculator on his head?

The Count!

NAMES

What do you call a man with some
cheese on his head?

Gordon Zola!

What do you call a man with a
bear on his head?

Teddy!

What do you call a woman with a
steering wheel on her head?

Carmen!

What do you call a teacher with
a joke book on his head?

A Tee-Hee-Cher!

What do you call a man with a
pile of chopped firewood on his head?

Axel!

What do you call a man with
a mortgage offer stapled to
his head ?

The Loan Arranger !

What do you call a man who forgets to put his
underpants on ?

Nicholas !

NAMES

What do you call a man with a tree growing
out of his head ?

Ed - Wood !

What do you call a woman with a sheep on her head ?

Baa - Baa - Ra !

What do you call a man who
wears tissue paper trousers ?

Russell !

What do you call a nun
with a washing machine
on her head ?

Sister Matic !

Why did the man with
a pony tail go to see
his doctor ?

He was a little hoarse !

What do you call a witch flying through the skies ?

Broom Hilda !

How did the Prime Minister get to know the secret ?

Someone Blairted it out !

What did the idiot call his pet zebra ?

Spot !

What do you call a fish on the dining table ?

A Plaice Mat !

What do you call a man made from toilet paper ?

Louie !

What do you call a very tidy woman ?

Anita House !

What do you call a vampire that can lift up cars ?

Jack - u - la !

What do you call a vampire in a raincoat ?

Mack - u - la !

What do you call a vampire Father Christmas ?

Sack - u - la !

HOOOO
HOOOO
HOOOO..

What do you call a girl who lives on the same
street as a vampire ?

The girl necks door !

What do you call a picture painted by an old master ?

An Old Masterpiece !

What do you call a horse that eats Indian food ?

Onion Bha - gee - gee !

What do you call a vegetable that tells jokes ?

Jasper Carrot !

What do you call the coldest mammal in the World ?

The Blue Whale !

What do you call a dog that makes a bolt for the door?

Blacksmith!

What do you call a man who steals cows?

A beef burgler!

What do you call a man with a pile of soil on his head?

Doug!

What do you call a man after he has
washed the soil off his head?

Douglas!

What do you call a girl at a railway station?

Victoria!

How does Posh Spice keep her husband under control?

He's at her Beckham call!

What do you call an overweight vicar who plays football?

The roly - poly - holy - goalie!

What do you call a woman with sandpaper on her head ?

Sandie !

What do you call her sister who lives at the seaside ?

Sandie Shaw !

What do you call the largest computer you can buy ?

A Big Mac !

What do you call medicine for horses ?

Cough stirrup !

What do you call a pretend railway ?

A play station !

What do you call a man with a kilt over his head?

Scott!

What do you call a man with a pig on his head?

Hamlet!

What do you call a man with eggs on his head?

Omelette!

What do you shout to the Frenchman
at the back of the race?

Camembert!

What do you call a poster advertising the
last teddy for sale in the shop?

A one ted poster!

REDUCED → LAST ONE ←

What do you call the dance that grown ups do
in the supermarket?

The can-can!

What do you call a DJ lying across a horse's back?

Jimmy Saddle!

What do you call a girl with a supermarket checkout on her head?

Tilly!

What do you call a mummy that washes up?

Pharaoh liquid!

What do you call a Scottish racehorse rider?

Jock - ey!

What do you call a pig with an itch?

Pork scratching!

What do you call a rodent's carpet ?

A mouse mat !

What do you call a sweater that bounces ?

A Bungee Jumper !

How do you spell hungry horse using just 4 letters ?

M T G G !

What do you call a woman dressed up as a gang of motor repairers ?

Car - men !

What do you call a Welshman who writes lots of letters ?

Pen Gwyn !

What sort of food can you get in a pub run by sheep ?

Baaa meals !

What do you call a female magician ?

Trixie !

What do you call well repaired holes in socks ?

Darned good !

What do you call a group made up of animal doctors ?

Vet, vet, vet !

What do you call a woman with a beach on her head ?

Shelly !

What do you call a postman with a cow on his head ?

Pat !

What do you call a woman who goes horse racing ?

Betty !

PHOTO FINISH

NAMES

What do you call a woman who works in a bakers ?

Bunty !

What do you call a dinosaur that drinks PG Tips ?

A Tea Rex !

What do you call a deaf monster ?

Whatever you like - he can't hear you !

What do you call a vampire pig ?

Pork-U-La !

What do you call a man with a collection of fish photographs ?

The Prints of Whales !

(Yes, I know they're *mammals* really, but
I liked the joke anyway !)

What do you call a man with this book on his head?

Joe King!

What do you call a man with a football pitch
on his head?

Alf Time!

What do you call a man who cleans out toilets?

Lou!

What do you call a man
with the word LATER
painted on his head?

Ron (Later Ron!)

What do you call a woman with a bicycle on her head?

Petal!

What do you call a woman with a computerised piano on the side of her head?

Cynthia!

What do you call a woman with a computerised piano on top of her head?

Hyacinth!

What do you call a man with a load of sports equipment on his head?

Jim!

What do you call a boy who is always making fun of people?

Mickey!

What do you call a man with a load of flowers and vegetables growing on his head?

Gordon!

What do you call a woman that people sit on?

Cher!

What do you call a man with a spade on his head?

Digby!

NAMES

What do you call a woman with a boat on her head ?

Maude !

What do you call a Roman emperor with flu ?

Julius Sneezer !

What do you call a man with a sack full of stolen goods over his shoulder ?

Robin !

What do you call a girl with a star on her head ?

Stella !

What do you call a mad man with the moon on his head ?

Lunar Dick !

What do you call a man with seagulls on his head ?

Cliff !

What do you call a secret store of food in a monastery ?

Friar Tuck

SECRET GRUB STORE

What do you call a man with a swarm of bees round his head?

A. B. Hive!

What do you call a woman with a short skirt on?

Denise!

What do you call a man with debts?

Bill!

What do you call a woman who throws her bills on the fire?

Bernadette!

What do you call a man who is part man, part jungle cat?

Richard the Lion Half!

Why did the girl have a horse on her head ?

Because she wanted a pony tail !

What do you call a man
with a karaoke machine ?

Mike !

What do you call a man who checks the size
of rabbit holes ?

A Burrow Surveyor !

What do you call a woman with a nut tree on her head ?

Hazel !

What do you call a failed lion tamer ?

Claude Bottom !

What do you call a woman with a cat on her head ?

Kitty !

What do you call a woman with a
food mixer on her head ?

Belinda !

What do you call a man who does everything in
30 seconds ?

Arthur Minute !

What do you call a woman who is crunchy and thin?

Crisp - tine!

What do you call a man who swings through the jungle backwards?

Nazrat!

What do you call a man who keeps chickens?

Gregory Peck!

What do you call a man with a computer on his head?

CD Ron!

What do you call a woman with a kettle on her head?

Tina!

What do you call a disguise worn by an Elk ?

A False Moosetache !

What do you call a robbery in China ?

A Chinese Take Away !

What do you call a cat that is always having accidents ?

A Catastrophe !

What do you call two elephants at the swimming pool ?

A Pair Of Swimming Trunks !

What do you call a dog in a breadcake ?

A Hot Dog !

What do you call a teddies favourite drink ?

Ginger Bear !

What do you call a dance that snowmen go to ?

A Snowball !

What do you call the ring that worms leave round the bath ?

The Scum Of The Earth !

What do you call a sheep that says Moo ?

Bilingual !

What do you call the flour that fairies make bread with ?

Elf Raising Flour !

What do you call the highest form of animal life ?

A Giraffe !

What do you call a snake that's good at maths ?

An Adder !

What do you call a secret agent in a shop ?

A Counter Spy !

What do you call a ghost that lives in a bicycle wheel?

A Spook!

What do you call a buffalo that you can wash your hands in?

A Bison!

What do you call a man who jumps off a cliff with a budgie on each arm?

A Budgie Jumper!

What do you call the glasses a short sighted ghost wears?

Spooktacles!

What do you call something that runs around your garden all day and never stops ?

The Fence !

What do you call the place where the Police keep rhubarb thieves ?

Custardy !

What do you call a frog's favourite sweet ?

A Lollihop !

What do you call something that is green and white and hops?

A Frog Sandwich!

UGH! That is so sick!

Yes, and so was my dad when he opened his packed lunchbox!

What do you call a holiday resort for bees?

Stingapore!

What do you call the song that monkeys and elephants sing at Christmas?

Jungle Bells!

What do you call a snail's favourite clothes ?

A Shell Suit !

What do you call a duck that's been to University ?

A Wise Quacker !

What do you call a baby turkey ?

A Goblet !

What do you call a rocking chair fitted with wheels ?

A Rock - And - Roller !

What do you call a pair of shoes made from
banana skins ?

Slippers !

What do you call first aid for an injured lemon ?

Lemonade !

What do you call Tarzan when he visits Mars ?

Marzipan !

What do you call a fish that's eaten 24 carrots ?

A Gold Fish !

What do you call a fish that can't swim ?

Dead !

What do you call the King who invented the fireplace ?

Alfred the Grate !

What do you call a cat that's eaten a lemon ?

A Sourpuss !

What do you say to an angry monster ?

No need to bite my head off !

What do you call the longest night of the year ?

A Fortnight !

What do you call a fast food snack served at
a church fete ?

A Hymn Burger !

What do you call a mayfly with criminal tendencies ?

Baddy long legs !

What do you call a ghost's songbook ?

Sheet Music !

What do you call a person who falls onto you
on a bus or train ?

A Laplander !

What do you call the World's first foot doctor?

William the Corncurer!

What do you call a holiday that rabbits go on when they first get married?

Bunnymoon!

What do you call a bull you can put in the washing machine?

Washable!

What do you call something purple that swings through vineyards ?

Tarzan the grape man !

What do you call a person who shouts all the way through a football match ?

A Foot bawler !

What do you call a fox in trouble with the police ?

A brush with the law !

What do you call a new, super cat ?

A Mew Improved Version !

ANIMALS

What do you have when a rabbit sits on your head?

A Bad Hare day!

What weighs two and a half tons, is grey, and floats
gracefully through the air ?

A Hang Gliding Elephant !

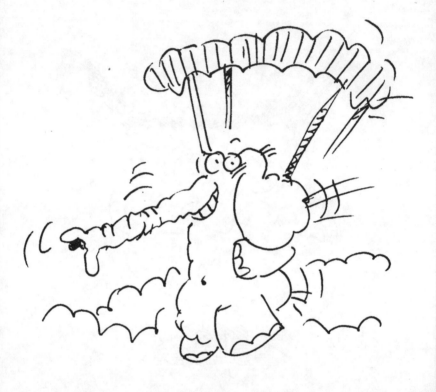

What's the worst thing about being a millipede ?

Washing your hands before tea !

A man went into a pet shop and asked the assistant if he could have a hamster for his son.

'Sorry, sir,' replied the assistant, 'we don't do part-exchanges.'

What did the earwig sing as it went to a football match ?

Earwig - go, earwig - go, earwig - go....

What is worse than finding a slug in your salad sandwich ?

Finding half a slug !

What do you call an 85 year old ant ?

An antique !

What happens when there is a stampede
of cows on the motorway?

There is udder chaos!

Where do you keep a pet vampire fish?

In your blood stream!

Have you ever hunted boar?

No, it's far too cold in this part of the world for that!

A cat just scratched my leg !

Shall I put some cream on it ?

No, it will be miles away by now !

What is big and grey and has yellow feet ?

An elephant standing in custard !

What is grey, has a trunk and travels at
125 miles an hour ?

A businessman on a fast train !

How did your budgie die ?

Flu !

Don't be daft, budgies
can't die from flu !

This one did - it flu
under a steam roller !

What fish can you
see in the sky ?

A Starfish !

Where do kippers go to be cured ?

They go to the local sturgeon !

Waiter - this crab only has one claw !

Sorry, sir, it must have been in a fight !

In that case, take this away and bring me
the winner !

Doctor, doctor, I think I'm a cat !

How long have you felt like this ?

Since I was a kitten !

What time is it when an elephant sits on your fence ?

Time to get a new fence !

Doctor, doctor, I think I'm a crocodile !

Don't worry, you'll soon snap out of it !

Who won the headless horse race ?

No one, they both finished neck and neck !

What do you call a worm in a fur coat ?

A caterpillar !

Help, I've lost my cat !

Well, why don't you put an advert in the local
newspaper ?

Don't be silly - cats can't read !

Eric, what is a prickly pear ?

Er....two porcupines ?!

Why do crabs walk sideways ?

Because they had to take some medicine which had side effects !

What sort of insects don't know the words to songs ?

Hum bugs !

..TUM-TE-TUM-TE-TUM....

A frog went to the doctor with a sore throat, the doctor examined him and said...'you've got a person in your throat !'

Where do ducks keep their savings ?

In river banks !

My dog often goes for a tramp in the woods - and the tramp is getting a bit fed up with it !

ANIMALS

What is the easiest way to get an elephant
to follow you home ?

Just act like a nut !

What do you call a dog that thinks it's a sheep ?

Baaaaaking mad !

What went into the lion's cage at the zoo and
came out without a scratch ?

Another lion !

First cow -   Are you worried about this mad
cow disease ?

Second cow - Doesn't worry me,
I'm Napoleon Bonaparte !

How do chimps make toast ?

Put it under a gorilla !

What goes bark, tick, bark, tick, bark, tick....

A watchdog !

What is grey and highly dangerous ?

An elephant with a hand grenade !

What did the dog say when its basket was
lined with sandpaper ?

Ruff, ruff !

How can you tell the difference between
an African elephant and an Indian elephant ?

Look at their passports !

What do you get when you cross a snake with
a magician ?

Abra - the - Cobra !

How many pigs do you need to make a smell ?

A Phew !

What is striped and keeps hearing a ringing sound ?

A zebra trapped in a telephone box !

What do ferrets have that no other creatures have ?

Baby ferrets !

What did the pig wear to the fancy dinner dance ?

A pig's - tie !

A man ran over a cat. He apologised to the owner and said that he would be happy to replace it !

'How good are you at catching mice ?'
the owner asked him !

How do you keep flies out of the kitchen ?

Put a load of manure in the dining room !

How can you cook chicken that really tickles
the palate ?

Leave the feathers on !

How does a horse tell a joke ?

In a jockey - lar fashion !

What do pigs call bath night ?

Hog wash !

How many sheep does it take to make a woolly cardigan ?

I didn't know sheep could knit !

How do snails get ready for a special night out ?

They put on snail varnish !

What do you get if a whale sleeps in your bed ?

A wet duvet !

What is a grasshopper ?

A cricket on a pogo stick !

Which insect can stay underwater for hours at a time ?

A spider in a submarine !

Robert, you can't keep a pig in your bedroom - what about the terrible smell ?

Don't worry, he'll soon get used to it !

Why do kangaroos hate bad weather ?

Because the kids have to play inside !

Why was your dog growling at me all through the meal ?

Don't worry, he always does that when people use his favourite plate !

What do you shout to rabbits getting on a ship ?

Bun - voyage !

When is a stray cat likely to come into your home ?

When you leave the door open !

Why did the girl have a pile of dirt on her shoulder ?

Because she had a mole on her cheek !

Waiter, waiter, what is this spider doing in my salad ?

Looking for the flies we usually have in there !

What happens when a frog breaks down ?

It gets toad away !

How do you stop a skunk from smelling ?

Put a peg over its nose !

What sort of animal are you never allowed to take into school exams ?

A Cheetah !

What's black and white and red ?

A zebra with nappy rash !

There's a stick insect in my salad - fetch me the branch manager at once !

How do you eat your turkey dinner ?

I just gobble it down !

Waiter, waiter, there's a button in my lettuce !

Ah ! That will be from the salad dressing sir !

What do monkeys do at the theatre ?

They ape - plaud !

Mmm ! This bread is lovely and warm !

It should be, the cat has been sitting on it
all afternoon !

How do you find a lost dog ?

Make a noise like a bone !

They make a perfect couple - He has a chip on his shouder, and there's something fishy about her !

What sound does a Chinese frog make ?

Cloak !

Where does a six foot parrot sleep ?

Wherever it wants to !

Is that a bulldog ?

No, it's a Labrador, but it ran into a wall chasing a cat !

What sort of dog has no tail ?

A hot dog !

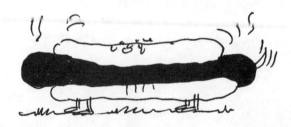

A man slipped when working on his roof, and was hanging onto the window ledge by his fingertips. He saw the cat through the window and called out to it to get help.

The cat said 'me ? how ?'

Why is a cat bigger at night than during the day ?

Because its owner lets it out at night !

What sort of jumpers do cows wear ?

Jerseys !

What do you get if you cross a skunk with a balloon ?

Something that stinks to high heaven !

What do cats read in the morning ?

The Mewspaper !

What did King Kong say when he was told that his sister had had a baby ?

I'll be a monkey's uncle !

What did the skunk say when the wind
changed direction ?

It's all coming back to me know !

What game do cows play at birthday parties ?

Mooo - sical chairs !

What game do cats play at parties ?

Puss - the - parcel !

What game do fish play at parties?

Sardines, what else!

What do you get if you cross a hippo with a house sparrow?

Massive holes in your roof!

Where would you find the skeleton of the very first, prehistoric cow?

In the Moooo-seum!

What did the sheep say to his girlfriend ?

I Love Ewe !

What did the short sighted hedgehog say to the cactus ?

Oh ! There you are mum !

What do you call a woman with a frog on her head ?

Lily !

What do you get if you cross a cow and a kangaroo ?

Something you need a trampoline to milk !

What is grey, has 4 legs and a trunk ?

A mouse going on holiday !

Did you hear about the stupid farmer who took his cows to the North Pole, thinking he would get ice cream !

What do you get if you cross a chicken with a dog?

Pooched eggs!

What is the closest thing to silver?

The Lone Ranger's saddle!

Look at those 50 cows over there!

I said, look at those 50 cows over there!!

Yes, I herd!

What sort of dog is good at looking after children ?

A Baby Setter !

What do the underwater police travel in ?

Squid cars !

Where do birds hold their coffee mornings ?

In a nest-cafe !

What sort of bird has fangs ?

Duckula !

What is hairy and writes ?

A ballpoint ferret !

What do you say to a hitch - hiking frog ?

Hop In !

I think your dog wants my dinner - he keeps jumping up at the table !

Well he didn't eat it this morning when I put it out for him so he'll have to do without now !

What do toads drink ?

Croaka Cola !

When do kangaroos propose ?

In Leap Years !

Why did the gorilla only eat one computer ?

Because he couldn't eat another byte !

What do you call someone who steals sheep ?

A Ram Raider !

Why is a real dog better than a cyberpet ?

Because your teacher will never believe you if you tell him that your cyberpet buried your homework in the garden !

How does the idiot call his dog ?

He puts both his forefingers in his mouth, takes
a deep breath, and shouts 'Here Boy.'

What sweet do lambs like best ?

A big baaaaa of chocolate !

On Christmas Eve a married couple were looking up into the sky at something travelling towards them.

Is it a snow storm ?, asked the wife

No, it looks like reindeer, replied the husband.

What do you do if an elephant sits in front of you at the cinema ?

Miss the film !

What did the Pink Panther say when he
stood on an ant ?

Dead ant, dead ant, dead ant dead ant dead ant...

What do elephants take to help them sleep ?

Trunkquilisers !

Where do tadpoles change into frogs ?

In the croakroom !

What did the dog say when it sat on some sandpaper ?

Ruff !

What do you call a delinquent octopus ?

A crazy, mixed -up squid !

What is the most cowardly farmyard creature ?

The Chicken !

What is the cheapest way to hire a horse ?

Stand it on four bricks !

What is the tallest yellow flower in the World ?

A Giraffodil !

What sort of bird steals from banks ?

A Robin !

What is green and white and hops ?

An escaping frog sandwich !

Why is an elephant like a teacher ?

Put a tack on an elephants chair
and you'll soon find out !

What do you call a stupid elephant with his own aeroplane ?

A Dumbo Jet !

Mary had a little lamb
the lamb began to tease her
'Stop it', she said,; the lamb refused
and now it's in the freezer !

When Mary had a little lamb
the doctor was surprised
but when old MacDonald had a farm
he couldn't believe his eyes

Why did the chicken blush ?

Because it saw the salad dressing !

What sort of animal does a ghost ride ?

A night mare !

How do ducks play tennis ?

With a quacket !

What do you get if you cross a hunting dog with a
newspaper writer ?

A newshound !

What do you call a large grey animal that's
just eaten a ton of beans ?

A smellyphant !

Why do bears have fur coats ?

Because they can't get plastic macs in their size !

Where is the hottest place in the jungle ?

Under a gorilla !

Two cows were talking in a field....

First Cow - Are you worried about catching this mad cow disease ?

Second Cow - Baaaa !

What is big and grey and good at sums ?

An elephant with a calculator !

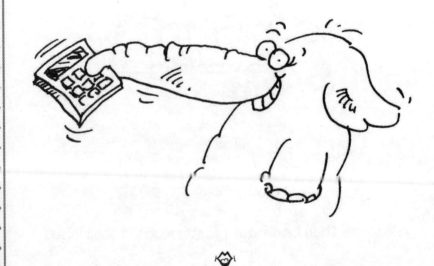

Why did the chicken run out onto the football pitch?

Because the referee whistled for a fowl!

Where do horses sit when they go to the theatre?

In the stalls!

Why did the chicken cross the playground?

To get to the other slide!

What ballet stars pigs ?

Swine Lake !

What do you do with a green elephant ?

Wait until he's ripe !

Why don't elephants eat penguins ?

They can't get the wrappers off !

What do sheep use to get clean ?

A Baaaa of soap !

What happened to the frog's car when it broke down ?

It was toad away !

What do you get if you cross a
crazy dog and a sheep ?

Baaaarrking mad !

Which is the trendy horse ?

The one with the pony tail !

THE COLOSSAL KIDS' JOKE BOOK

What says Moo, Baaa, Woof, Quack, Meeooow, Oink ?

A sheep that speaks foreign languages !

What animals with a cold do the police use ?

Sniffer dogs !

Where would you find a martian
milking a cow ?

In the milky way !

What is the best way to get in touch with a fish ?

Drop him a line !

Good morning Mr Butcher - do you have pigs' trotters ?

No, I always walk like this !

What do you get if you cross a pig with a millipede ?

Bacon with legs !

Where do rabbits learn to fly helicopters ?

In the hare force !

Why can't I get the King of the jungle
on the telephone ?

Because the lion is busy !

What was the name of the woman who crossed the
Gobi desert on a dromedary ?

Rhoda Camel !

Why does a flamingo lift up one leg ?

Because if it lifted them both up it would fall down !

What grows down as it grows up ?

A Goose !

Where would you hear fowl language on a farm ?

Outside the chicken coop !

My mum and dad said my new boyfriend isn't fit to live with pigs !

What did you say to that ?

I stuck up for him, I said of course he is !

Why do elephants have trunks?

Because they would never fit their huge clothes into a suitcase!

When do lions have twelve feet?

When there are three of them!

First leopard - Hey, is that a jogger over there?

Second leopard - Yes, great, I love fast food!

Johnny - Mum, is our dog metric ?

Mum - Why do you ask ?

Johnny - Because Dad said it has just had a litre of puppies ?!

What is round, brown, smelly and plays music ?

A cowpat on a record player !

When do you know you have chicken pox ?

When you are constantly feeling peckish !

What is black and white and gets
complaints from all the neighbours ?

A Zebra learning to play the drums !

How can you get eggs without chickens ?

By keeping geese and ducks !

Why should you be naughty if you have
a cow for a teacher ?

Because if you are good you might
get a pat on the head !

I've lost my dog !!

Why don't you put a card in the
post office window ?

Don't be stupid - he can't read !

What is a polygon ?

An escaped parrot !

Where do cows go for their holidays ?

Moo York

or

Patagonia

or

Uddersfield !

Who cuts a sheep's hair ?

The Baaarber !

Where do farm animals keep their savings ?

In a Piggy bank !

What is it called when a cat falls from the farmhouse roof and smashes all the glass in the greenhouse ?

A Catastrophe !

First goldfish –   I told you we'd be famous one day –
                    and now it's going to come true !

Second goldfish – Wow! When is all this going to
                    happen ?

First goldfish –   They're putting us on the television
                    tomorrow !

What do you call an insect that has
forgotten the words ?

A Humbug !

Why do octopuses never get mugged?

Because they are always well armed!

What do pussy cats read with their mice crispies?

Mewspapers!

If spiders live in Crawley and bees live in Hastings, where do hares live?

On your head!

What did the idiot call his pet zebra ?

Spot !

How do frogs send messages to each other ?

Morse Toad !

What game do skunks play ?

Ping Pong !

What was the first motorised vegetable called ?

The Horseless Cabbage !

I'd like a pair of gloves for my dog, please.

What breed is he ?

A Boxer !

What do cows eat for breakfast ?

Moosli !

THE COLOSSAL KIDS' JOKE BOOK

Why are cows rubbish at maths ?

Because they haven't invented the cowculator yet !

What television channel do wasps watch ?

The Beee Beee Ceee !

Why do some animals wear cowboy boots in the jungle ?

Because they go lion dancing !

ANIMALS

Where are all the aspirins in the jungle?

There aren't any - the paracetamol!

What was the 30 metre tall Monopoly box
doing in the jungle?

It was a big game hunter!

What do country and western singers
wear in the jungle?

Rhino-stones!

What is the first thing Tarzan puts on in the morning ?

His jungle pants !

What were Tarzan's last words ?

Who put grease on this vine ?!

Why don't leopards bother to cheat in exams ?

Because they know that they will always be spotted !

Why was the zebra put in charge of the jungle army ?

Because he had the most stripes !

What is smelly and has no sense of humour ?

A dead hyena !

What do you call a well dressed jungle cat ?

A dandy lion !

Where does a horse stay on holiday ?

In the bridle suite !

What is cold, furry and minty ?

A Polo Bear !

Where would you find a 10,000 year old cow ?

In a Moooseum !

What sort of sheep stick to the bottom of boats >

Baaaaanacles !

As sheep don't have money, how do they buy and sell ?

They have a baaarter system !

Why did the sheep buy a hotel ?

He's always wanted to own a baaa !

What do cows put on in the morning ?

Udder pants !

How do you control a horse ?

Bit by bit !

Why was the young horse sent out of the classroom ?

He was acting the foal !

Doctor, doctor, I'm turning into a young cat !

You must be kitten me !

What sort of jokes do chickens like best?

Corny ones!

(which is why we sell so many copies
of this book to chickens!)

Where do rodents go for holidays?

Hamster Dam!

Why do cats always finish the job?

Because they purr - severe!

Where do cats go when they die ?

The the Purrr - ly gates !

Where do rodents go for holidays ?

Hamster Dam !

What was the name of the horse that fought windmills ?

Donkey Oatey !

What sort of music do you hear most in the jungle ?

Snake, rattle and roll !

How can you travel through the jungle at
60 miles an hour ?

Inside a cheetah !

What do Tigers use to wake up in the morning ?

A Llama clock !

What is the difference between a buffalo and a bison ?

You can't wash your face in a buffalo !

What sort of flowers do monkeys grow ?

Chimp - pansies !

When cows play football, who has the whistle ?

The Heiferee !

Why don't farmers allow sheep to learn karate ?

Because their chops would be too hard !

What do you get if you cross a tortoise with a bird ?

A Turtle dove !

What was the name of the famous French cow painter ?

Too moos Lautrec !

What does a sheep call members of his family ?

Sheepskin !

How do you know when a dog has been naughty ?

It leaves a little poodle on the carpet !

What do you call an electronic dog ?

An Interpet !

Why don't elephants use computers ?

Because they are scared of the mouse !

EEK!

If you give a mouse gorgonzola
cheese what will happen ?

Your computer will smell !

Why did the pony keep coughing ?

He was a little hoarse !

What do sheep do on sunny days ?

Have a baa baa cue !

My daughter took her pet sheep to
the local sports day. '
Is he a good jumper ?,' someone asked her.
'Not yet,' she replied !

Why don't cows sunbathe ?

Because they don't want to tan their hides !

Why did the astronaut jump onto the cows back ?

He wanted to be the first man on the Moo !

What do they call it when an insect kills itself ?

Insecticide !

What do you get if you cross a baby with a porcupine ?

A lot of problems changing nappies !

Why did the idiot take salt
and vinegar to
the zoo ?

**To put on the
chippopotamus !**

What do you call an elephant
that's also a
witch doctor ?

A Mumbo - Jumbo !

Why are elephants such bad dancers ?

Because they have two left feet !

ANIMALS

Why do bat mums and dads always
complain about their kids ?

Because all they do is hang around all day !

What did the Boa-constrictor say to the explorer ?

I've got a crush on you !

Which creature builds all the houses in the jungle ?

The Boa-constructor !

What did the first Piranha say to the second ?

I've got a bone to pick with you !

What do jungle police officers drive ?

Panda cars !

What did the first Piranha say to the second ?

I've got a bone to pick with you !

Where is it not safe to park in the jungle ?

On a double yellow lion !

What do you do if you fancy a bite in the jungle ?

Kick a lion up the backside !

Which bird is good at chess ?

The Rook !

Why is it hard to fool a stick insect ?

Because they always twig !

What are baby stick insects called ?

Twiglets !

Why did the stick insect go to university ?

He wanted to branch out !

Two baby skunks - called In and Out - went out for a walk one day. In got lost, but his brother soon found him. How ?

In - stinkt !

How would you sell a cow's home ?

You would need to find a byre !

What did the farmer say when the townie asked him if he had any hay ?

Stacks !

What sort of music does a
gifted rodent write ?

Mousterpieces !

Baby snake - **Dad, are we poisonous ?**

Dad snake - **No, son, why do you ask !**

Baby snake - **I've just bitten my tongue !**

What do they sell at Tarzan's takeaway ?

Finch, Chimps and mushy Bees !

What do you get if you cross a kangaroo with a kilt?

Hop Scotch!

What is a sheep's favourite wine?

Lambrusco!

What do you give a budgie with constipation?

Chirrup of figs!

What kind of fish do pelicans like?

Any kind - as long as they fit the bill!

What is sheepskin useful for ?

Keeping the sheep's inside where they belong !

What sort of wallpaper do birds like best ?

Flock !

Why do farmers keep cows ?

Because there are no udder animals
as good at giving milk !

How do elephants change their car wheels if
they have a puncture ?

They lift it up with a jackal !

What bird is always running out of breath ?

The Puffin !

How do you stop a skunk from smelling ?

Tie a knot in his nose !

ODDS AND ENDS

Why are you taking that shovel to your singing class?

So I can get to the low notes!

What do you call a an underwater spy ?

James Pond !

What sort of dancing will elephants
do in your front room ?

Break dancing !

Knock, knock...
Who's there ?
Boo.
Boo who ?
No need to get upset, it's just a game !

Where would you find a rubber trumpet ?

In an elastic band !

What time is it when you have
eaten half of your lunch ?

Half ate !

Doctor, doctor...
I feel like the man in the moon !
What has come over you ?
A cow !

What sort of car is a Rolls-Canardly ?

A car that rolls down hills
but can hardly get up them !

What is a duck filled fatty puss ?

An overweight cat that has just eaten a duck !

How do electricians get over high fences ?

They volt !

I asked for vegetarian sausage –
these are made from beef !

But the cow was a vegetarian !

Where does Father Christmas go
for his Summer holidays ?

Santa Maria !

Hello, Carol, how was your first day at school ?

First – you mean I have to go back again ?!

Did you hear about the cowboy who used to
sit up all night making models of cows
from tissue paper – he was
sacked for rustling !

How do they recycle old bicycles ?

A man ran into a bar and got three fractured ribs...

...it was a steel bar !

A man wanted to be a lumberjack...
He flew out to Canada and bought a chainsaw and got a job. At the end of the first week he had cut down 100 trees. 'That's not enough,' said the foreman, 'we expect you to cut down at least 200.'
However, he offered to buy the man's chainsaw to help with his air fare home.
"I'll just test it first,' said the foreman, and started the engine.
'How do you get it to make that noise?' said the man !?

When do you change the water in a goldfish bowl ?

When they've drunk the first lot !

What do ghosts shout at a bad play ?

Booooooooooooo !

What do skeletons say after they've
seen a really good play ?

That was a rattling good show !

How does Jack Frost get about ?

By Icycle !

What do you call a travel agent in the jungle ?

A Trip - opotamus !

What drink do Australian bear manufacture ?

Coca - Koala !

Which animal tells the best jokes ?

A stand -up chameleon !

What's the quickest way to get out of the jungle ?

By ele - copter !

What sort of poetry is known everywhere ?

Uni - verse !

My Dad must be the greatest magician ever –
yesterday he turned his car into a side street,
and the day before he turned it
into a lay-by !

Waiter – where's my elephant sandwich ?

Sorry, Sir, I forgot !

What do bogey men drink ?

Demon – ade !

Who do female ghouls get married to ?

Edible batchelors !

What prize is awarded each year to the best dieter ?

The No – Belly Prize !

Nurse - can you take this patient's temperature please ?

Certainly doctor - where to ?

Before you give anyone a piece of your mind -
check to make sure you will have enough
left for yourself afterwards !

What's round, shiny, smelly and comes out at night ?

A foul moon !

Does Cyclops get a television licence at half price ?

Are my indicators working ?

On and off !

Why is that farmer setting fire
to the plants in his field ?

He's growing baked beans !

Why did you give up your job as a fortune teller ?

To be honest I couldn't see any future in it !

How do you know if a Boa-constrictor loves you ?

It will have a crush on you !

Why do boxers like going to parties ?

They love to get to the punch !

How do you know where an
escaped train is hiding ?

Just follow the tracks !

What sort of boats do clever
schoolchildren travel on ?

Scholar - ships !

Who runs the pub in the jungle ?

The wine-ocerous !

Knock, knock...
Who's there ?
Alison.
Alison who ?

Alison to you asking me that question every day !

What game do prisoners like best ?

Cricket - they like to hit and run !

ODDS AND ENDS

Knock, knock...
Who's there ?
Alpaca.
Alpaca who ?
Alpaca suitcase and leave if you keep
asking these silly questions !

What do you get if the central heating goes
haywire in a pet shop ?

Hot dogs !

Which vegetable is best at snooker ?

The Cue - cumber !

What do you call a man who preserves pears ?

Noah !

What did the artists say when he had to
choose a pencil ?

2B or not 2B, that is the question !

How do you know when your dustbin is
full of toadstools ?

Because there's not mushroom inside !

What do you get if you cross a cow with a monster ?

A horrible mootation !

Why did the stick insect cover himself with marmite ?

He was going to a fancy dress party as a twiglet !

Which ancient leader invented the cruet set ?

Sultan pepper !

Is that bacon I smell ?

It is and you do !

What is a robot's favourite snack ?

Nucler fission Microchips !

What do you do with a ladder in
a hot country ?

Climate !

What runs round the garden without
ever getting out of breath ?

The fence !

What do you call a man who looks at the
sky all night long ?

A night watchman !

What animal lives on your head?

The hare!

Did you hear about the robot policeman?

He was a PC - PC!

And - did you hear about the mechanical writer?

Robot Louis Stevenson!

Where do monsters go fishing?

Goole!

Why did the idiot try to spread a goat on his toast?

Because someone told him it was a button!

ODDS AND ENDS

Where should you send a one-legged,
short sighted man ?

To the hoptician !

What do you get if you cross a bird with a frog ?

Pigeon toed !

What is the difference between a mad rabbit
and a forged £50 note ?

One is a mad bunny, the other is bad money !

Doctor, are you sure it's my arteries that
are the problem ?

Listen I'm a doctor, aorta know !

When is a King like a book ?

When he has lots of pages !

Why did the jelly wobble?

Because it saw the milk shake!

Water - A colourless liquid that turns brown when you put your hands into it!

Why did the idiots stand in an open doorway?

They wanted to play draughts!

Why didn't the idiot's home made airbag stop him from breaking his nose when he crashed?

He didn't have enough time to blow it up!

ODDS AND ENDS

Where do very tough posties sleep ?

On pillow boxes !

Why were the judge and jury on a boat ?

Because the prisoner was in the dock !

What sort of food is made from old Chinese boats ?

Junk food !

What do you call a happy crocodile with a camera ?

Snap happy !

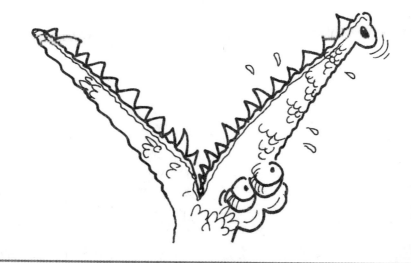

Why are so many famous artists French ?

Because they were born in France !

Why did the American Indian chief put
smokeless fuel on the fire ?

He wanted to send some secret messages !

What goes up a drainpipe down but
can't come down a drainpipe up ?

An Umbrella !

What did the paper say to the pencil?

You lead me astray!

Why do wolves howl at the moon?

Because they have such rotten singing voices!

Did you hear about the man who drove round telling everyuone he was rich and successful, when he was actually a failure?

He was a mobile phoney!

Why was the poor dog chasing his tail?

He was trying to make ends meet!

How do you know when you come to the end of a joke book?

Because there's no more laughing matter!